Here may we prove the power of prayer
To strengthen faith, and sweeten care;
To teach our faint desires to rise,
And bring all heaven before our eyes.

—*William Cowper*

To my wife and children

PRAYING
TOGETHER

KINDLING PASSION FOR PRAYER

UPDATED AND REVISED EDITION

JAMES BANKS

Discovery House.
from Our Daily Bread Ministries

Praying Together:
Kindling Passion for Prayer

©2009, 2016 by James Banks

Formerly titled *The Lost Art of Praying Together*

Discovery House is affiliated with Our Daily Bread Ministries, Grand Rapids, Michigan.

Requests for permission to quote from this book should be directed to: Permissions Department, Discovery House, P.O. Box 3566, Grand Rapids, MI 49501, or contact us by e-mail at permissionsdept@dhp.org.

All Scripture quotations, unless otherwise indicated, are taken from the Holy Bible, New International Version®, NIV®. *Copyright* © 1973, 1978, 1984, 2011 by Biblica, Inc.™ Used by permission of Zondervan. All rights reserved worldwide. www.zondervan.com. The "NIV" and "New International Version" are trademarks registered in the United States Patent and Trademark Office by Biblica, Inc.™

ISBN: 978-1-62707-491-9

Interior design by Melissa Elenbaas

Printed in the United States of America
First printing of this edition in 2016

Contents

Introduction

Imagine that one day you received an invitation in the mail. It simply said, "I'd love to meet with you and a few friends." It gave a time and a place—later in the week at the church you attend. And it was signed, "Jesus."

Let's assume for just a moment that you had no reason to question whether the invitation was real (let's just say that heaven has a stamp and a postmark, and they're both on the envelope). How would you respond? Wouldn't you want to go?

Jesus promised that "where two or three gather in my name, there am I with them" (Matthew 18:20). That verse, along with others in God's Word, present a special invitation to us. God invites us to meet with Him in a unique and powerful way when we pray together. When Christians seek His face together, Jesus, by a new and living way, opens the curtain of the Most Holy Place, and beckons us to come in (Hebrews 10:19–25).

The thought of praying with others might make you a little uncomfortable. I understand.

Most of us feel inadequate when it comes to prayer, and even more so when it comes to praying with others. But God never intended prayer to be something reserved for the "super spiritual." He longs for us to come to Him and welcomes us even when we hardly know what to say. When hearts are humbled in sincere, honest prayer before Him, Jesus draws near. And that changes everything.

I learned that from personal experience.

When I was twelve years old, my family moved inland from the booming San Diego area to the rural desert of Southern California. We left a vibrant, growing church of nearly two thousand members for one with fewer than fifty. And it was there that I encountered God's presence in a way I never had before.

My parents came to the church because of the youth ministry, but it was the praying that would change my life. There was the row of little old ladies with "blue" hair in the next-to-last pew who prayed me through my adolescence. And when I left home for Germany, they wrote me to let me know their praying hadn't stopped. There were the pastor and his wife who had come out of retirement to serve the church, who took the time to listen to whatever questions I had (I had a lot of them) and to sit down in a quiet corner and pray with me. There was old Mr. Gibbs, who took me and my best buddy Aaron fishing on Saturdays. On Sundays, he quietly interceded with Bob Offe and Jim Strain and others for special needs in the front of the church. I can still hear their voices, loving God and encouraging one another as they prayed.

It took a while for me to comprehend that there was power in that little desert church, despite its size. Like Jacob waking up, over time I would come to understand that the Lord was in this place, and "I was not aware of it" (Genesis 28:16). The lasting impact God made on my life through the members of that little church was in direct proportion to their loving prayers.

Look through the Old and New Testaments, and you'll discover the unique blessings God offers to people when they pray together. Whenever something significant happens in the history of the church—whenever lives are transformed and awakening occurs—people are praying together.

That's why this book was written—to encourage those who know they need to pray and to give them the tools and support they need to help them pray effectively. The first four chapters of this book underscore the priority that God places on praying together in His Word. Once the biblical foundation is set, the remaining chapters provide time-tested, practical insights to encourage individuals, families, and churches as you pray. Each chapter concludes with "Prayer Confidence Builders" and "Questions for Reflection" that can be used in a small group or for personal study. You also won't want to miss the appendices at the end of the book, which include guides to help new prayer groups get started and several other useful tools. For other helpful resources on prayer, please visit my website at JamesBanks.org and Discovery House at dhp.org.

God bless you as you read! He has already promised to bless you as you pray. May this book encourage more prayers to rise "like incense" (Psalm 141:2), so that together we may enter into the wonder of what only God can do.

1

Me? Pray with Others?

Accepting the Invitation

Prayer moves that arm which moves all things else.

C. H. Spurgeon

Me? Pray out loud? I get nervous when I try to pray in front of other people."

Jim was trying to find a nice way to say no to my invitation to the prayer meeting that night, and I knew exactly how he felt.

I love to pray with others, but it wasn't always that way. There was a time when just the mention of prayer meetings brought up not-so-spiritual memories of "praying without ceasing," trying helplessly not to look at my watch as seconds ticked slowly by.

Let's be honest. Prayer meetings aren't at the top of most people's lists of favorite things to do, and there's a reason. Praying together is a lost art for many Christians. Not only are we not used to doing it, we feel awkward when we try. Sometimes we let a few less-than-inspiring experiences discourage us. We can even feel that it's only something reserved for a select group of Christians, those who are "good" at praying or who have the "spiritual gift" of prayer.

Nothing could be further from the truth. Search God's Word, and you'll never find prayer mentioned once as a spiritual gift set aside for a select few (check out 1 Corinthians 12:7–10 and Romans 12:6–8 for lists of the gifts of the Spirit). God wants every believer to pray. He loves it when we do and wants our prayers together to be a constant source of life-transforming encouragement and hope. God has great plans for our prayers, and our "skill" at prayer has nothing to do with it. His strength "is made perfect in weakness," and He waits to show us what He will do when our eyes are on Him alone (2 Corinthians 12:9). True prayer has much more to do with God's faithfulness in response to waiting hearts than with our ability to string words together.

God's Spirit is sparking new interest in praying together today, and that's exciting. Four hundred years ago, Puritan pastor Matthew Henry wrote, "When God intends great mercy for a people, the first thing He does is set them a-praying."[1] Amazing things happen when God's people pray! When we pray together, our heavenly Father invites us into the wonder of watching Him work and offers us a front-row seat. God waits for us to claim His special promises for people who pray.

Music to Our Father's Ears

Jesus promised in Matthew 18:19, "If two of you on earth agree about anything they ask for, it will be done for them by my Father in heaven." He makes it clear that *when we pray with others*, we capture God's attention in a special way.

The word *agree* that Jesus uses is from the Greek *sumphoneo*, the root of our English word *symphony*. That word points to the truth that our prayers together are beautiful music to God.

Imagine a concert where God is in the audience, just waiting for His children to begin. Our heavenly Father looks forward to our prayers together and hears them with a deep sense of satisfaction because of His love for us. It doesn't matter how our praying may sound to our own ears. Think of parents at an elementary school concert just waiting to hear their children's first awkward notes. Our praying together is as imperfect as we are, but God smiles with approval. We may not even feel like anything is happening, but our united prayers are deeply moving to God. So moving that I could pray a lifetime on my own and never come close to what may happen when I pray with others. The Bible tells us that "the prayer of a righteous person is powerful and effective" (James 5:16). But imagine what the prayers of *many* can accomplish, offered with faith in Jesus's promise that God hears and answers in a special way when we pray together.

It may be no coincidence that the culture we live in has become increasingly indifferent and even hostile to Christianity at the same time that united prayer has gone out of the church. As recently as fifty years ago, prayer meetings were a vital part of many churches. As American culture became increasingly entertainment oriented, the midweek prayer meeting began to be replaced by other Wednesday night activities. Over time, the prayer meeting moved out of the sanctuary and into a corner of the church library (if it happened at all). At the same time, the church's impact upon the culture around us began to gradually decline.

But you can make some great discoveries in church libraries. Dust off a few old books, and you'll discover that a church without prayer is a church without power. Prayer infuses the church with power and makes the smallest church a David to the world's Goliath. As the British poet William Cowper wrote over two hundred years ago:

Restraining prayer, we cease to fight;
Prayer makes the Christian's armor bright;
And Satan trembles when he sees
The weakest saint upon his knees.[2]

There is no greater need in the church today than for Christians to rediscover the importance of praying together. Go back to earlier days, and you'll find God's people hungering for the chance to pray. They gave prayer a huge priority in their lives, and because they did, God enabled them to accomplish more than they ever could have achieved in their own strength.

Praying together changes history. The First Great Awakening, which started in America and Britain in the 1730s, began to stir a few years earlier with Moravians on their knees in Germany, praying for the spread of the gospel around the world. The Second Great Awakening, which swept through the United States with revivals and camp meetings beginning in 1800, followed an organized effort by Jonathan Edwards to unite God's people in prayer on both sides of the Atlantic. The Third Great Awakening was sometimes called "The Prayer Meeting Revival" because it started with a series of meetings in New York City in 1857, which spread throughout the country and profoundly influenced lives wherever they went (including that of evangelist D. L. Moody).

Praying together takes patience and practice. But whenever God breathes new life into His people and His church, somewhere, someone is praying. C. H. Spurgeon captured this principle well over 150 years ago when he wrote, "All through the church of God the true progress is in proportion to the prayer."[3]

What Are We Missing?

When we skip praying together, we miss out on the chance to see the difference between what we can accomplish and what only God can do. Bill Hybels wrote, "When I work, I work. But when I pray, God works."[4] When we pray we draw close to God's heart and tap into His infinite power and love. God has chosen to use our prayers—especially our prayers together—as one of the main ways

He accomplishes His work in our world. That may be why the first request of the Lord's Prayer is for His kingdom to come (Matthew 6:10; Luke 11:12). God has chosen our prayers as one of the main means by which His work moves forward.

In May of 1934 in Charlotte, North Carolina, a small group of friends met together on a dairy farm to pray. It was the middle of the Great Depression, and the farmer had lost all of his savings in the banking collapse the previous year. But he gave up much-needed time at work that day to pray with his friends.

Together they asked God to raise up a person from the Charlotte area who would share the good news of Jesus all over the world. A few months later, the farmer's teenage son (who was mocking his father's friends at the time of the prayer meeting by referring to them as "fanatics") committed his life to Jesus during an evangelistic campaign. His name was Billy Graham.[5]

You have to wonder what would have happened if there hadn't been a small prayer meeting on the Graham farm that day. What would we have missed? How many millions of people would never have heard the message of Jesus's love through the sermons of Billy Graham if this small group of faithful believers had not asked God to intervene?

The strategy of the devil is to divide and conquer. Ours is a distracted age where people go through increasingly isolated lives separated from God and each other in a never-ending quest for self-fulfillment. Depression, substance abuse, narcissism, and random acts of violence decry the desperation of our times, and it's easy to feel as if our adversary has the upper hand.

God's Word reminds us that the devil is a defeated foe. Christ, "having disarmed the powers and authorities, . . . made a public spectacle of them, triumphing over them by the cross" (Colossians 2:15). The One who is in us "is greater than the one who is in the world"

(1 John 4:4). He calls us to "approach God's throne of grace with confidence, so that we may receive mercy and find grace to help us in our time of need" (Hebrews 4:16). When God's children seek Him together on their knees, His power and love flow through us in ways that go far beyond our ability to ask or understand.

God deeply desires for us to pray together. The night before Jesus was crucified our unity was so important to Him that He prayed for it more than anything else (John 17:11). It was in those moments He also asked, "Couldn't you men keep watch with me for one hour? . . . Watch and pray so that you will not fall into temptation" (Matthew 26:40–41).

Henry Blackaby writes, "I think God is crying out to us and shouting, 'Don't just do something. Stand there! Enter into a love relationship with Me. Get to know Me. Adjust your life to Me.'"[6] Our heavenly Father invites us to join Him on the greatest adventure of our lives. If we take Him up on it, He promises that He will not only show us things we never thought were possible, He will also give blessings we never even considered asking for.

The New Testament tells us that God is "able to do immeasurably *more* than *all we* ask or imagine, according to his power that is at work within *us*" (Ephesians 3:20, emphasis added). Those words *ask* and *imagine* are plural: The idea here is that we will be asking and imagining *together,* which was the earliest practice of the church, where "they all joined together constantly in prayer" (Acts 1:14). And because His power is at work within *us*, our loving and faithful Father is waiting for us to seek Him together so that He can work through us and move in ways that reach far beyond anything we could conceive of on our own.

Asking Our Father to Help Us

Imagine you're watching two children doing their best to move a rock in their backyard.

"Push!" They yell encouragement to each other, but the rock won't budge.

Their father is also watching, a few yards away.

"One . . . two . . . *three!"* They try again. But no matter how much they push, they get nowhere.

"Have you tried everything you could?" Dad asks.

"Everything!" they yell back exhausted. "We can't do it! We've tried and tried, and it's just too big!"

"There is one thing you haven't tried," Dad says gently, with a smile in his voice.

"What's that?"

"You haven't asked me to help you."

I've *lived* that story. As a pastor and church planter serving active churches, I found myself continually on the lookout for the next "big idea." There was no shortage of glossy mailers filled with programs, enough to keep me and the churches I served occupied with activities for years to come (or at least until we stumbled upon "the next big thing"). There was just one problem.

We hadn't asked our Father to help us. Not really. Sure, we had prayed. Every board meeting started with prayer. But then we got on with "the business" of the church, relying more on our own strength than God's.

George Barna surveyed several hundred senior pastors to determine their top three ministry priorities. Discipleship and spiritual development ranked highest (47 percent listed it as a priority). Evangelism and outreach were also right up there (46 percent). Preaching rounded out third place (35 percent). Prayer wasn't even in the running. Only 3 percent of pastors listed it among their primary priorities for ministry.[7]

Something is desperately wrong with those numbers. In many respects, the church is better equipped today than we ever have been in history. We have technology, talent, multimillion dollar facilities, and a plethora of plans and programs. Yet even a quick look around reveals that for all of these advantages, our influence on lives and hearts in the culture around us has waned significantly.

But God is faithful. Interest in prayer and praying together is on the rise, and that's a good thing. There is a growing hunger to see what God alone can do above and beyond our ability to plan or program. A fresh wind of the Spirit is blowing, removing the dust that has long covered the lost art of praying together. That's exciting.

This isn't a book about the past. It's about the good things God *will* do when His people pray. What could be more exciting than seeing heaven touch earth in response to our prayers, a front-row seat to a fresh move of God? Imagine the changes we could see in our lives and the lives of those we love if we responded to God's invitation to meet Him in prayer!

An Opportunity Not to Be Missed

John Holecek attended the first church I served right out of seminary. John is a bold believer whose life was radically turned around by God. A prodigal son come home, he went from drug abuse and a long "walk on the wild side" in the 1960s to smuggling Bibles behind the Iron Curtain at the height of the Cold War.

One Sunday morning John and I were talking after worship when someone approached us and began to share a problem. I was responding with a rather pious sounding, "I'll pray for you" (meaning later, on my own, if I remembered), when John jumped on the moment: "Yes! Let's pray right now! That way we won't forget to do it later!" He quietly bowed his head and prayed aloud, caring for the person and her need in a thoughtful and practical way. God marked that moment in my mind, teaching me a lesson I will remember as long as I live. *Prayer with others is an opportunity that is not to be missed.*

I hope you won't miss it as long as I did. Learning to pray with others has been a slow work of grace in my life. It didn't come naturally for me, and I still have a lot to learn. But God is faithful. He continues to surprise me with His kindness, presence, and power. The truth is that some of the sweetest moments of my life have been spent praying with others.

If you hunger to see what only God can do in response to prayer, this book is for you. If you feel inadequate when it comes to praying, you'll also find help here. We'll take a fresh look at what the Bible says about praying together in both the Old and New Testaments. We'll rediscover what Jesus taught about praying with others, including a life-changing promise He made to those who pray that is often overlooked. We'll look at the priority the early church placed on united prayer and unearth inspiring examples of God's people praying together throughout history. And we'll discover some simple, time-tested ideas for praying with others that can help us personally experience God's presence and power *today* beyond all "we ask or imagine" (Ephesians 3:20)

When we pray together, God invites us on an adventure into His goodness and love where we and those around us may be deeply blessed.

The adventure awaits! There are breathtaking discoveries to be made along the path of praying together. Our prayers together are even a preview of heaven itself, where "a great multitude that no one could count" will bow before the Lamb (Revelation 7:9–10).

God's promises for people who pray together are beyond counting. His Word through the prophet Jeremiah speaks to the moment:

> Stand at the crossroads and look;
>> ask for the ancient paths,
>> ask where the good way is, and walk in it,
>> and you will find rest for your souls. (Jeremiah 6:16)

Untold blessings await those who walk with God on the path of prayer. The journey opens before you, and God is holding out His hand.

Prayer Confidence Builder #1

Our confidence in praying with others grows as we take time with God in prayer on our own. As a way of preparing to spend time with others in prayer, schedule a specific time to pray on your own. During that time, ask God to help you learn how to pray and to show you places in your life where you can begin to pray with others.

Questions for Reflection or Discussion

1. What comes to mind when you think of prayer meetings? Have you ever attended a prayer meeting? What was it like?

2. What did Jesus say about the importance of praying together in Matthew 18:19? Do you ever draw a correlation between praying together and God answering prayer?

3. Do you agree that Christian influence on society has decreased since churches have stepped away from prolonged prayer together? Why or why not?

4. What role does heartfelt, united prayer play in your personal life? In the life of your church?

5. Do you see praying together as an opportunity or a burden? Why do you see it that way?

A Closer Look at a Lost Art

Finding Help in Unexpected Places

Men, great and influential in other things but small in prayer, cannot do the work Almighty God has set out for His church to do in this, His world.

E. M. Bounds, *The Weapon of Prayer*

On September 11, 2001, my wife, Cari, and I held an emergency prayer meeting in our home. Members of our church dropped what they were doing and filled our living room that evening as we prayed for our nation and the victims of the World Trade Center tragedy. A half hour into the meeting, there was a knock on the door. It opened to a man we had never seen before.

"I saw the cars," he said. "I knew you were a pastor and thought you might be praying. I hope you don't mind if I join you. *I just feel like I have to pray . . .*"

People were driven to pray after September 11. Attendance at worship services spiked across the country. Prayer meetings and vigils occurred coast to coast. As footage from the collapse of the Twin Towers aired hourly and the toll in human lives mounted, a sense of foreboding hung in the air. The magnitude of the tragedy made us realize that our best help could be found only through prayer.

Prayer as a "First Resort"

Prayer in the Old Testament was often like that. Insurmountable circumstances forced God's people to turn to Him. As they did, they discovered how deeply He cared for them and how powerfully He would move when they called on Him from the heart.

God never intended praying together to be a last resort. He promises to be "near to all who call on him" and tells us, "Never will I leave you; never will I forsake you" (Psalm 145:18; Hebrews 13:5). God is *always* available, waiting for us to call on Him. The infinite wisdom and resources of our heavenly Father stand poised and ready to be released when we wait before Him in prayer.

That raises a life-changing question: What if we made praying a "first resort"? What if we were more proactive about prayer? What if we made a habit of praying more often? What blessings might we receive that we wouldn't experience if we didn't ask? What positive, heaven-sent changes would occur? Our heavenly Father tells us, "Call to me and I will answer you and tell you great and unsearchable things you do not know" (Jeremiah 33:3). We don't know the difference our prayers will make until we really begin to pray.

A story is told of a woman who had just arrived in heaven. An angel is showing her around when she notices a number of beautiful gold boxes, each with a name embossed in elaborate lettering.

"What are those?" she asks. "Is there one with my name?"

"There is," the angel replies, "but you might not want to look inside."

"Why is that?"

The angel gives her a kind and knowing glance: "Because it contains all of the blessings God was waiting for you to ask for on earth. But you never asked."

What if we *did* ask?

God has showed us in His Word that He will do beautiful and unexpected things in response. When we begin to take that to heart, we'll be encouraged to give prayer a new place in our lives as well.

In the pages that follow, we'll take a sweeping look at what God did whenever His people made a genuine effort to join together and pray. The Old Testament contains many poignant examples of why praying together matters. But some of them also happen in unexpected places. Let's go there first.

Praying Together in Unexpected Places

It doesn't really look like a prayer meeting, and it happens in a surprising place. One of the earliest prayer meetings in the Bible occurs when Moses, Aaron, and Hur are standing on a hill overlooking the battle as Joshua leads Israel against the Amalekites. The seventeenth chapter of Exodus describes what happened throughout the day:

> As long as Moses held up his hands, the Israelites were winning, but whenever he lowered his hands, the Amalekites were winning. When Moses' hands grew tired, they took a stone and put it under him and he sat on it. Aaron and Hur held his hands up—one on one side, one on the other—so that his hands remained steady till sunset. So Joshua overcame the Amalekite army with the sword. (vv. 11–13)

Why was Moses holding up his hands? Moses was doing more than just holding up his staff. The staff represented the power of God. Moses was raising the staff before the Lord of heaven's armies, asking for His help. When he lacked the strength to stand, Aaron and Hur held Moses's arms before God and struggled for His blessing together.

Aaron and Hur holding Moses's arms up before God paint a powerful picture of prayer. When people prayed in the Old and New Testaments, their most common posture was standing with their hands upraised (Deuteronomy 32:40; Psalms 28:2; 63:4; 119:48; 134:2; Lamentations 2:19; 3:41; 1 Timothy 2:8).

The Bible tells us that Moses was a mighty intercessor. The book of Exodus even records how "the LORD *relented*" from destroying Israel when Moses interceded for them (Exodus 32:14, emphasis added). Moses's prayers changed the course of history. And if you take a closer look, you'll also notice that often Moses didn't act alone. The Old Testament records the Lord speaking "to Moses *and* Aaron" at least seventeen different times between Exodus, Leviticus, and Numbers. Moses and Aaron were frequently in God's presence *together*, and their prayers made a powerful impact.

Facedown in Prayer

One surprising example of Moses's and Aaron's intercession occurred during the rebellion of Korah. When Korah's followers were challenging Moses's authority, the Lord threatened to destroy the entire assembly of Israel yet again. But Moses's and Aaron's prayers together caused God to relent in a way that seemed to change His mind. (Numbers 23:19 tells us that God *does not* "change his mind," but our prayers together often lead us to a deeper realization of what God actually intends. God allows for the interaction of His will with our own when we pray, and powerful things happen! More on this in chapter 10.) No matter how we may understand it theologically, the biblical and practical truth is that their prayers together made an incalculable difference in the lives of the people they led and served.

When Moses and Aaron interceded for their people, they "*fell facedown* and cried out, 'O God, the God who gives breath to all living things, will you be angry with the entire assembly when only one man sins?'" (Numbers 16:22, emphasis added). Falling facedown was a way of praying with humility, and whenever you see God's people doing this in the Old Testament, they are praying together. After Israel's unexpected loss at Ai, Joshua "*fell facedown* to the ground before the ark of the LORD, remaining there till evening. *The elders of Israel did the same*, and sprinkled dust on their heads" (Joshua 7:6, emphasis added). The same thing happened when God disciplined David for taking a census. He and the elders of Israel, "clothed in sackcloth, *fell facedown*" (1 Chronicles 21:16, emphasis added). When Ezra (who led the first group of exiles back to Israel from Babylon) was burdened by his people's sin, he "was praying and confessing, weeping and *throwing himself down* before the house of God." A large crowd of men, women, and children gathered around him and wept as well (Ezra 10:1–2, emphasis added).

In each instance, God moved mercifully in response to His children's heartfelt confession, repentance, and prayer.

Days of Prayer

The Old Testament also tells us about days of prayer when the entire nation of Israel waited before God. On the brink of civil war during the period of the judges, "the Israelites went up and wept before the LORD until evening, and they inquired of the LORD" (Judges 20:23). On another occasion, David assembled "all Israel" for a joyful celebration in worship and prayer when the ark was brought to Jerusalem after it had been captured by the Philistines (1 Chronicles 15:3). Solomon did the same thing for the dedication of the temple (1 Kings 8:2). Years later, when the book of the law was discovered in the temple, Josiah called together "all the elders of Judah and Jerusalem" and renewed the covenant "in the presence of the LORD" (2 Chronicles 34:29–31). A National Day of Prayer was a well-established practice in the history of Israel!

Fasting and Praying Together

God's people also prayed together with fasting. When the Jews were in danger of annihilation during their exile in Persia, the situation changed only after Esther asked her people to hold a prayer meeting and intercede for her: "Go, gather together all the Jews who are in Susa, and fast for me" (Esther 4:16). Fasting was always accompanied by prayer.[1] Ezra also called for a time of fasting and prayer in Babylon by the Ahava Canal before Israel's journey out of exile, "so that we might humble ourselves before our God and ask him for a safe journey for us and our children" (Ezra 8:21). Another time, when the Israelites resettled their homes under Nehemiah's leadership after years of exile, they spent a day together before God fasting and confessing their sins to Him (Nehemiah 9:1–2).

Help When All Seems Lost

Just as the events of September 11 resulted in a new passion for prayer in our nation, times of crisis often brought God's people to their knees. Israel cried out to God when they were oppressed in Egypt and later during the period of the judges.[2] Three tribes of Israel called on God in the heat of battle, and "He answered their prayers, because they trusted in him" (1 Chronicles 5:20). When Judah was surrounded by invading armies, Jehoshaphat proclaimed a fast and the people "came together to seek help from the LORD; indeed, they came from every town in Judah to seek him" (2 Chronicles 20:4). People of all ages prayed for God's mercy on their nation. Second Chronicles points out that "all the men of Judah, with their wives and children and little ones, stood before the LORD" (20:13).

When it seemed all hope was lost, God's people discovered His unconquerable strength as they waited on Him in prayer again and again. King Hezekiah and Isaiah the prophet cried out to God together when the Assyrian king Sennacherib laid siege to Jerusalem, and God intervened miraculously (2 Chronicles 32:20). Daniel also asked his three friends to pray when his life was in danger so he might gain the wisdom he needed to interpret Nebuchadnezzar's dream. All of their lives were saved as a result (Daniel 2:17–18).

The Secret of Strength

Christians from previous generations have learned a lot from the time-honored Old Testament practice of praying together. One of them was Charles Haddon Spurgeon, pastor of the Metropolitan Tabernacle in London during the latter part of the 1800s (one of the first megachurches in the English-speaking world). Spurgeon made the discovery that praying together was the secret of his church's success through the years. He compared it to the secret of Samson's strength and warned against ever stepping away from it:

> The prayer-meeting is an institution which ought to be very precious to us, and to be cherished very much by us as a Church, for to it we owe everything. When our

comparatively little chapel was all but empty, was it not a well-known fact that the prayer meeting was always full? And when the Church increased, and the place was scarce large enough, it was the prayer meeting that did it all. When we went to Exeter Hall, we were a praying people, indeed; and when we entered on the larger speculation . . . of the Surrey Music-hall, what cries and tears went up to heaven for our success! And so it has been ever since. It is in the spirit of prayer that our strength lies; and if we lose this, the locks will be shorn from Samson, and the Church of God will become weak as water.[3]

Samson discovered that God alone is the real source of strength. When we pray together we make the same discovery in heartfelt and exciting ways.

The Promise of Praying Together

One of the greatest minds of colonial America, Jonathan Edwards, encouraged believers on both sides of the Atlantic to pray fervently in a "concert" of prayer (meaning, a "concerted effort"). Edwards beautifully described the wonder of what happens when Christians sincerely pray together: "It is one of the most beautiful and happy things on earth, which indeed makes earth most like heaven" (see appendix 5 for more information on how to have a concert of prayer similar to the ones Edwards encouraged).[4]

Wouldn't you love to see heaven touch earth again and again? Wouldn't you love to see lives and hearts transformed by what God alone can do?

You're about to. Praying together in the Old Testament sets the stage for what is about to happen as God's Spirit is poured out on

His people in the New Testament. God was preparing to release His presence and power in a way that had never happened before, a way that would change history forever.

God promised through the prophet Isaiah, "My house will be called a house of prayer for all nations" (Isaiah 56:7). Jesus quoted this Scripture the day He turned over the tables in the temple court-yard. Jesus was also about to turn the tables on the way God's people pray together. *He* made a promise that would change *everything*.

In the next chapter, we'll take a closer look at that promise. We'll discover *why* praying together matters so much to Jesus and why it should matter to us.

Prayer Confidence Builder #2

Schedule another time to pray, just as you did in Prayer Confidence Builder #1. Find a quiet place where you can be alone with God, where no one can hear you but Him. As you pray, pray aloud. Talk to God as if He were sitting right beside you, or place an empty chair in front of you and talk to God as if He were sitting in the chair. You will find that praying aloud helps you focus your thoughts and keeps your mind from wandering. It will also help you be more comfortable and natural when praying aloud with others.

Questions for Reflection or Discussion

1. If you had a box in heaven of prayers that were unanswered because they were unasked for, what would be in it?

2. Explain how Moses, Aaron, and Hur were actually praying when Israel fought the Amalekites (Exodus 17). What was a common posture of prayer in the Old Testament?

3. What was Moses's and Aaron's body language before God when they interceded in prayer during the rebellion of Korah (Numbers 16)? Why is this actually praying?

4. What did Daniel ask his three friends to do when his life was in danger? What did God do as a result?

5. Why did Spurgeon compare praying together to the secret of Samson's strength?

6. What is a "concert of prayer"? How did Jonathan Edwards describe united prayer?

3

Where Two or More

Praying with Jesus

It is Christ, praying Himself, who teaches us to pray.

Andrew Murray,
With Christ in the School of Prayer

One summer Sunday morning I was visiting family in California when I found myself at The Church On The Way in Van Nuys. It was an early service and I went on my own, taking a seat toward the back where I could slip out quickly enough if I wanted to.

I have to admit that I went to worship that morning with a spectator mentality. The church was internationally known for its gifted and influential pastor. I had heard about the ministry for years, and it was my first visit. I was curious about what God was doing there, trying to learn anything I could to take back to my church at home. But while I was looking for the next "big idea," God had something better in mind.

Toward the beginning of the worship service, Pastor Jack Hayford turned to the congregation and said, "This is the time where we pray for each other. I'd like to ask you to turn to a couple of people beside you and bring any concerns you may personally have before God together."

Something inside of me tensed. I had been expecting your usual pastoral prayer, where I could sit passively and listen while someone else talked to God. Instead, I was being asked to pray myself, and to even open up to total strangers. I was thinking about slipping out of the pew when the lady sitting beside me smiled kindly in my direction. Suddenly the man sitting behind us asked, "Can I pray with you?"

I was caught, and there was no turning back.

The young man behind me was a Korean student. He began to speak very candidly about a sin he was struggling with in his personal life. The lady beside me was black with a gentle Jamaican accent. She listened thoughtfully and then earnestly shared a sincere personal need. Their honesty was so disarming, I found myself opening up about a sin in my own life. Moments later, we were all bowing our heads.

What followed seemed a little like heaven. As we quietly began to pray, I could hear the gentle buzz of voices around the room. I could sense that something significant was happening, something words cannot quite capture.

It was the unmistakable touch of God's presence. It seemed as if Jesus himself were walking up and down the aisles of the church, ministering to people in a deeply personal way. It was a genuinely holy moment, and it caught me entirely by surprise.

I can't tell you anything else that happened that morning. I don't remember the sermon or a single song. But that quiet moment in prayer stays with me.

In this chapter, we'll catch a glimpse of what it must have been like to pray with Jesus. We'll look at what Jesus taught and practiced when it came to praying with others. We'll even discover how it is possible to pray with Him today.

When Jesus Prayed with Others

For years, when I imagined Jesus praying, I thought of Him only withdrawing to lonely places to pray (Luke 5:16). It was later I realized that was just a small part of the picture. As I began to search the New Testament, I discovered that Jesus loved to pray with others. We see that from the sheer number of times the Bible tells us He did it. How had I overlooked it so long?

It happened when He "took Peter, John and James with him and went up onto a mountain to pray" (Luke 9:28). He taught the Lord's Prayer to the disciples after they were watching Him pray and one of them asked Him to "teach us to pray" (Luke 11:1). Jesus also prayed with others at His baptism and His transfiguration (Luke 3:21; 9:28–29). If the disciples hadn't been listening to Jesus pray and John hadn't written down His words, we would have no idea how fervently Jesus prayed for everyone who would ever believe in Him (John 17:1–26). John also records Jesus's prayer in the presence of Lazarus's family and friends in the moments before He raised Lazarus from the dead (John 11:41), so that the people there would benefit by believing. Prayer flowed naturally from Jesus. He lived in prayer, staying in constant communication with the Father wherever He went.

You can discover more about how much Jesus wanted His followers to pray together when you take a closer look at the Lord's Prayer. Notice that it's an "us" prayer and not a "me" prayer ("*Our* Father . . . Give *us* today our daily bread." [Matthew 6:9, 11, emphasis added]). Jesus begins the Lord's Prayer by saying "This, then, is *how* you *should* pray" (Matthew 6:9, emphasis added). Jesus is not only telling us what to pray for, He's telling us *how* He expects us to pray. Because the language of the prayer is plural, the natural meaning of Jesus's words indicates that His followers will be praying *together*. Daniel Henderson observes: "The pronoun here is plural, so He is talking about a group—the disciple group. In our language it would be 'when you guys pray' or 'when y'all pray' (in Southern dialect). In other words, Jesus says, 'When you all pray together as my followers, do it this way . . .'"[1] The grammar indicates that Jesus is assuming His followers will be praying *together*.

Jesus's priority on praying with others is shown clearly through the fact that it was what He wanted to do most in His final moments on earth. The long night before His crucifixion, Jesus prayed alone and urgently asked others to join Him. His convicting words to Peter and the other disciples (when He came back and found them sleeping) are penetrating reminders of how much it meant to Him: "Couldn't you men keep watch with me for one hour? . . . Watch and pray so that you will not fall into temptation. The spirit is willing, but the flesh is weak" (Matthew 26:40–41).

What about Praying in Front of Others?

An important question needs to be asked. Didn't Jesus caution against praying in front of others? Haven't we all heard others use praying together as a platform to pontificate their own pious views?

Yes and yes. But that's not all there is to it.

You might look at Jesus's encouragement to pray in private and think He's advising against *any* kind of public prayer. Here's what He said: "But when you pray, go into your room, close the door and pray to your Father, who is unseen. Then your Father, who sees what is done in secret, will reward you" (Matthew 6:6).

Does this mean that Jesus is saying we shouldn't pray with others at all?

Take a closer look at the chapter of Matthew in which those words occur, and you'll notice that what Jesus is really after is our *motives* when we pray. The chapter begins with Jesus cautioning His listeners to "be careful not to practice your righteousness in front of others to be seen by them" (Matthew 6:1). He warns us not to announce our giving to the needy "with trumpets" and tells us not to be "like the hypocrites," who "love to pray standing in the synagogues and on the street corners to be seen by others" (Matthew 6:2, 5). What Jesus is after here is any kind of disingenuous display of "righteousness" that is intended to call attention to ourselves, instead of sincerely seeking after God.

Jesus wants His followers to have the same down-to-earth humility and dependence in prayer that He demonstrated. Our prayers and our relationship with God need to be real in private before they can be expressed in public. *If Jesus had been against praying with others, He would not have done so personally on so many different occasions.*

Andrew Murray, a nineteenth-century South African pastor, gives a beautiful explanation of the balance of Jesus's private and public prayer life: "As a tree has its root hidden in the ground and its stem growing up into the sunlight, so prayer needs secrecy in which the soul meets God alone, *and* it needs public fellowship with those who find their common meeting place in the name of Jesus Christ."[2] Trees send down deep roots, where no one can see, and draw life, nourishment, and strength from the soil. But the most beautiful and productive part of the tree is its leaves, bark, and branches, which cannot remain hidden for the tree to survive and thrive. Jesus prayed privately because He was dependent on God. But He also prayed frequently with others as well, and His actions provide the model for all believers to follow.

The Helplessness of Jesus

Jesus shows us that the deepest meaning and purpose in life are found in being *completely dependent* upon God. "The Son can do nothing by himself," Jesus said. "He can do only what he sees his Father doing" (John 5:19).

We don't usually think of Jesus saying something like "I can do nothing," but it was in this humble reliance on the Father that He showed His greatest strength. As God incarnate, Jesus could have been the most independent person who ever lived. Yet His life was marked by a dependence on God that stands in stark contrast to the maverick kind of self-reliance so highly regarded by our culture today.

Ole Hallesby, a Norwegian Christian imprisoned by the Nazis during World War II, wrote, "True prayer is a fruit of helplessness and faith. Helplessness becomes prayer the moment that you go to Jesus and speak candidly and confidently with Him about your needs. This is to believe."[3]

This is the "helplessness" Jesus demonstrated throughout His life on earth. The more demands for His time and attention, the more He sought the Father's guidance and strength. Jesus's complete reliance on God is demonstrated in the amount of time He spent in prayer on His own and with others and establishes the pattern of prayer for every believer who would follow Him.

Daniel Henderson explains, "Prayer in its simplest definition is depending on God. When we do not pray, we are saying, 'Lord, I think I can live the Christian life on my own.' Prayerlessness is our 'declaration of independence' from God."[4] Sometimes we go through our daily lives with actions that say, "I'm just fine on my own, thank you." Not that we would ever tell God that, but when we forget to pray or rely on prayer as a last resort, we're missing out on something very special in our relationship with Him.

Jesus showed us that we're most effective when our lives are given over to Him moment by moment: "I am the vine; you are the branches. If you remain in me and I in you, you will bear much fruit; apart from me you can do nothing" (John 15:5). He explains clearly that just as He could do nothing apart from the Father, we can do nothing apart from Him. When we are connected to Him through dependent prayer, our lives receive fresh meaning and direction as we are caught up in His purposes. The success of everything we do as believers depends on this, because only then are we functioning in Jesus's strength and not our own.

One promise Jesus made underscores this more than any other.

The Promise

Jesus promised that *"where two or three gather in my name, there am I with them"* (Matthew 18:20, emphasis added). It's one of the most compelling promises in all of God's Word. But it's also frequently misunderstood.

For years, I thought these words from Jesus simply meant that any time a few Christians got together, He would be there in a general, spiritual sense. After all, His Spirit dwells in all believers, so He would naturally be wherever they are. Comforting and true as that is, it isn't what Jesus is promising here.

Take a closer look at these words, and you'll notice that Jesus is describing people who are coming together *for the specific purpose of prayer.* To understand His promise correctly, we have to read this verse along with the one that occurs before it: "Again, truly I tell you that if two of you on earth agree about *anything they ask for,* it will be done for them by my Father in heaven. ***For*** *where two or three gather in my name, there am I with them* (Matthew 18:19–20, emphasis added). That little word *"for"* is a coordinating conjunction (which also occurs in the original Greek) that implies a direction connection with the verse immediately before it. It indicates that when we seek God in humble, believing prayer together, Jesus promises His presence in a unique and powerful way. The prefix for the word for "coming together" in this verse is also a root of our English word *synergy*, which may be defined as the whole being greater than the sum of the parts. What happens when Christians pray together is more than just subjective experience or the "warm fuzzies" of human togetherness. The Spirit of God is at work in a special way that is different from His work in any other actions that Christians undertake, even individual prayer. When we meet as one to reach for God's will and purposes together, Jesus makes His presence *known*.

This isn't something mystical or out of reach of the experience of ordinary people (the disciples *were* ordinary people [Acts 4:13]), but it is something that is spiritually discerned (1 Corinthians 2:14). In *Fresh Wind, Fresh Fire*, author and pastor Jim Cymbala includes a comment from a minister who visited the Brooklyn Tabernacle one Sunday morning, illustrating this point well: "You can tell how popular a church is by who comes on Sunday morning. You can tell how popular the pastor or evangelist is by who comes on Sunday night. But you can tell how popular Jesus is by who comes to the prayer meeting."[5]

People make one of the most exciting discoveries of the Christian life when they recognize the presence of Jesus among them when they pray together. Jan was a member of our church who was undergoing chemo for breast cancer. But she faithfully attended our prayer meetings. One night when we prayed for her, she said, "I don't know what will happen; but whatever happens, I know that all will be well. He was *here* tonight." Stay in prayer with others long enough, and you'll find yourself making the same discovery: Jesus is *here*.

For centuries, Christians have affirmed Jesus's special presence when they pray together. One notable example was Evan Roberts, a leader in the powerful nineteenth-century revival that transformed Wales. Roberts resolved in his diary to "remember Thomas," and "never miss a prayer meeting."[6]

Thomas wasn't with the other disciples when Jesus first appeared to them after the resurrection, and he missed out on being with Him. Roberts felt he *had* to be where people were praying because Jesus's presence had become so real to him there. The fact that Jesus was there brought deep comfort to his faith and filled him with a sense of anticipation for what God would do next.

God with Us, Then and Now

Whatever century we live in, Jesus will always be Immanuel, "God with us" (Matthew 1:23). When the earliest Christians made this discovery, it changed the world.

Andrew Murray observed, "Jesus never taught His disciples to preach, only to pray."[7] In the pages that follow, we'll find out *why*.

Prayer Confidence Builder #3

The more we learn to pray spontaneously on our own, the more comfortable we'll feel praying with others. This week, try to spend more time praying "in the moment" than you ever have before. Make an extra effort to be especially attentive to persons and situations around you as they open up opportunities for prayer. For example, when you hear a siren, pray both for the people in need and for those trying to help them. If you anticipate having a difficult day at work, pray about it before you arrive. Or if you have the opportunity to witness a sunset, take a moment to praise God for it.

Questions for Reflection or Discussion

1. What are some examples of Jesus praying with others in the New Testament?

2. How does the Lord's Prayer provide instruction for people to pray *together*?

3. When Jesus cautioned against praying in front of others, was He against any kind of public prayer? What was He talking about?

4. Andrew Murray compared a Christian's prayer life to a tree. What did he mean?

5. How did Jesus demonstrate helplessness while He was on earth?

6. Why is Jesus uniquely present when Christians pray together?

4

Catching the Wind
The Early Church at Prayer

We cannot organize revival, but we can set our sails to catch the wind from Heaven when God chooses to blow upon His people once again.

G. Campbell Morgan

Nobody likes to wait, but that is exactly what Jesus told the disciples to do the day He ascended into heaven: "Do not leave Jerusalem, *but wait* for the gift my Father promised" (Acts 1:4, emphasis added).

Waiting isn't easy. Neither is living apart from Jesus once you know who He is. Imagine how the disciples felt. For three years they had the privilege of brushing shoulders with the miracle of God in the flesh, day and night. John gives us a hint of what this was like: "We have seen his glory, the glory of the one and only Son, who came from the Father, full of grace and truth" (John 1:14).

But now He was gone, and they didn't know when they would be with Him again.

We know what happened next, because the Bible tells us in detail. But the disciples had to live the long hours between Jesus's ascension and the outpouring of the Holy Spirit on the day of Pentecost. It wasn't easy.

There were so many questions: *Jesus told us not to leave Jerusalem. How long will we have to wait? What is the gift the Father promised, and how will we know when it comes? When will we see Jesus again?* Even though Jesus had explained much, there was much they only recognized after the fact.

As soon as Jesus ascended into heaven, the disciples went to the upper room. We can only imagine what their conversation was like.

Imagine them sitting around the same table where they shared the Last Supper. As the memories come flooding back, one by one, they begin to speak . . .

"Remember when Jesus raised Lazarus from the dead?" John asks.

"What about the time He fed that crowd of over five thousand people?" Mark recalls, still amazed as he remembers the extra baskets of food they gathered after everyone had been fed.

"Or when He showed up *alive* on the road to Emmaus, and our friends didn't even recognize Him!" Luke adds.

A slow smile crosses Matthew's face. "That makes me wonder. Maybe we're missing something again. Something important. *Remember?* Remember what Jesus told us? *'Where two or three gather in my name, there am I with them'* (Matthew 18:20, emphasis added). He told us to wait, and there's something we need to do while we're waiting. If we *pray,* He *will* be with us! Maybe Jesus isn't as far away as we thought!"

Of course the Bible doesn't tell us exactly what they said in those moments, but Luke carefully records how Jesus's followers spent their time for the next forty days: *"They all joined together constantly in prayer,* along with the women and Mary the mother of Jesus, and with his brothers" (Acts 1:14, emphasis added). We *know* that while they were waiting for God's next move, they decided that the best thing they could do together was *pray.*

The First Act of the Apostles

The first act of the apostles was to pray. The more they prayed together, the more they experienced God's presence and blessing in ways they hadn't expected.

The disciples prayed because they were doing what Jesus told them to do and were depending on His promises to them. Jesus had told them to wait. Jesus had promised He would be with them when they prayed and had also assured them, "I will not leave you as orphans; I will come to you" (John 14:18). Jesus had also given them instructions during the forty days before He ascended into heaven, and it shouldn't be missed that the very first thing they did as soon as they returned to Jerusalem was pray (see Acts 1:3–14). It wasn't long after they began to pray that they saw the promise of His presence fulfilled in a remarkable way with the outpouring of the power of the Holy Spirit on the day of Pentecost (Acts 2:1–4).

We're about to take a quick glance through the New Testament at how much prayer mattered to the first Christians. But be advised. Their passion for prayer is contagious. And if we learn to pray like they did, it will change us. It will also change the world.

Devoted to Praying Together

The first believers prayed together with urgency. After the Holy Spirit descended on the day of Pentecost, Luke tells us they "*devoted themselves* to the apostles' teaching and to fellowship, to the breaking of bread and *to prayer*" (Acts 2:42, emphasis added). They prayed together when choosing a replacement apostle to fill the space that Judas had left (Acts 1:24). The first miracle in the church occurred as Peter and John were on their way to pray together at the temple (Acts 3:1–10). When they were thrown in prison afterward, they held a prayer meeting as soon as they were released. "After they prayed, the place where they were meeting was shaken" (Acts 4:23–24, 31). You begin to see a pattern. The apostles began to pray, and God showed up.

God waited for the first Christians to pray and moved miraculously in response. It was as if He were teaching them to walk, holding out His arms as they moved forward, step by step. Cries of prayer have been called the "growing pains" of the church, a sign that God is moving among His people.[1] As the number of believers increased, the apostles chose others to assist with necessary tasks, explaining that they would give their "*attention to prayer* and the ministry of the word" (Acts 6:1–4, emphasis added). Prayer became a priority for them, just as it was for Jesus.

Praying First, Acting Later

The early church prayed first and then acted (instead of deciding what they wanted to do and then asking God to bless it). The first missionaries were commissioned at a prayer meeting—the Holy Spirit directed the early church to send Barnabas and Paul after a time of united fasting and prayer (Acts 13:3). The first worship service in Europe started spontaneously as a prayer meeting, when Paul and his companions were on their way to a "place of prayer" in Macedonia (Acts 16:13–15). For the first three hundred years, the early church had no formal buildings, no personal Bibles, no multimedia displays, and no surround sound systems. But they prayed persistently, and God moved as a result.

When Peter's life was in danger after Herod threw him in prison, the church had a late-night prayer meeting to intercede for him and received a response so immediate they had trouble believing it! Peter's first action when he was set free was to seek out the home of John's mother, "where many people had gathered and were praying" (Acts

12:1–17). When Paul and Silas were thrown in prison in Philippi, they responded with a midnight prayer meeting, and God shook things up again—with an earthquake (Acts 16:25–28).

Praying Together as a Matter of Survival

Beyond Acts, there are many more references throughout the New Testament that suggest how much praying together mattered for the earliest Christians. Paul, Silas, and Timothy wrote the church in Thessalonica, "We always thank God for all of you and continually mention you in our prayers. We remember before our God and Father your work produced by faith" (1 Thessalonians 1:2–3). Paul and his missionary companions chose praying together as a way of blessing others and showing them how much they loved them. Even when there were differences of opinion, such as when the believers in Tyre tried to persuade Paul not to go on to Jerusalem, Luke writes that their response was to seek God's blessing together in prayer: "All of them, including wives and children, accompanied us out of the city, and there on the beach we knelt to pray" (Acts 21:5).

Paul and Timothy credited their survival to the prayers of others. Writing about a difficulty they faced in Asia (what is today Turkey), where they felt "the sentence of death" in their hearts, Paul and Timothy wrote that "this happened that we might not rely on ourselves but on God" (2 Corinthians 1:9). They told the church in Corinth, "On him we have set our hope that he will continue to deliver us, *as you help us by your prayers.* Then many will give thanks on our behalf for the gracious favor granted us *in answer to the prayers of many*" (2 Corinthians 1:10–11, emphasis added).

The lives of the earliest Christian missionaries depended moment by moment on the faithful prayers of others. No wonder Paul insisted on praying so much and told the church to "pray without ceasing"

(1 Thessalonians 5:17 NKJV). He had discovered the difference God makes when we seek Him together on our knees.

Praying Together: Priority One

Paul's advice to Timothy shows the priority he placed on prayer for all believers: "I urge, then, *first of all,* that petitions, prayers, intercession and thanksgiving be made for all people" (1 Timothy 2:1, emphasis added). He then adds, "I want the men everywhere to pray, lifting up holy hands without anger or disputing" (1 Timothy 2:8). If Paul were encouraging men everywhere to pray alone, he wouldn't have added "without anger or disputing"; if they were praying alone, there would be no opportunity for "anger or disputing" because there would be no one to fight with! Even when they didn't get along, the earliest believers were to make praying together a priority. Peter encouraged husbands to treat their wives with respect, "so that nothing will hinder your prayers" (1 Peter 3:7). Married or single, praying together mattered.

James, the brother of Jesus, also underscores the importance of a life rich in prayer: "Is anyone among you in trouble? Let them pray. Is anyone happy? Let them sing songs of praise. Is anyone among you sick? Let them call the elders of the church to pray over them" (James 5:13–14). James knew that when we pray together transparently and humbly, God moves in powerful, personal ways: "Therefore confess your sins to each other and pray for each other so that you may be healed. The prayer of a righteous person is powerful and effective" (James 5:16). When God's people pray, He draws us into His presence, and we are blessed.

The Difference Prayer Makes

It was prayerfulness that God noted as the difference between the unconverted "Saul" and the converted "Paul." When the Lord told Ananias in a vision to visit Saul, Saul's willingness to pray was the defining characteristic God used to describe the change that had occurred: "Go . . . for he is praying" (Acts 9:11). Samuel Chadwick, in his classic book *The Path of Prayer*, beautifully describes how God used prayer to transform Saul of Tarsus's life:

> It brought a new assurance of God, a new confirmation of faith, a new fellowship of the people of God, a new experience of healing, a new vocation, a new inheritance, a new power. Prayer changes things. Prayer makes all things possible, for it links the praying soul to the omnipotence of God.[2]

Their Secret Source of Strength

The early church changed history in a way we would love to see happen today. Armin Gesswein explains why:

> The church *was* the prayer meeting. The entire assembly was at prayer . . . What is the story of this Jerusalem church? It is the story of one small praying congregation of about 120 members in an upper room in the city of Jerusalem which got on fire for God and went on to change the world![3]

God moves when people pray together. Even the smallest group of people can make a God-sized impact for good in the world through their prayers. But if we don't pray, we'll see little change. C. H. Spurgeon put it well: "How could we expect a blessing if we were too idle to ask for it? How could we look for a Pentecost if we never met with one accord, in one place, to wait on the Lord? . . . We shall never see much change in our churches in general till the prayer meeting occupies a higher place in the esteem of Christians."[4]

No human effort can accomplish what God can do when He is sincerely invited to move in power in the lives of His people. As John Piper wryly points out, "God looks on the heart, and knows the difference between the lifted sails of prayer and the outboard motor of human method."[5]

Treasured by God

The New Testament tells us our prayers are treasured by God. Revelation lifts the curtain of heaven with a beautiful picture of "the prayers of all God's people" blended together in "golden bowls," rising like incense before the Father's throne (5:8; 8:3–4).

Incense was precious in the ancient world. Prayer is likewise precious to God; He values it as a deep expression of the love and dependence of His people. Few things are as pleasing to God as the aroma of the prayers of His people, kept before Him constantly. It is significant that the prayers are kept together, and not separately. The unity of His children has always mattered to God.

The early church learned through experience that when they went to God together in prayer, come what may, everything that followed was better.

If you want to see God move in ways you never imagined, step out on the adventure of praying with others! Make it a priority, and pray with urgency and boldness. God waits for Christians to humble themselves in prayer together so that we may rely on His strength and He can respond with power and love. When we spread the sails of prayer to catch the wind of His Spirit, who knows where He will take us?

Prayer Confidence Builder #4

Thanking and praising God is an important and encouraging part of praying with others. Try practicing this in your personal prayer time. Begin by listening to a favorite hymn or song of praise, and then spend some time expressing your love and gratitude to God through your prayers. Begin silently, and then express your praises aloud.

Questions for Reflection or Discussion

1. What did the disciples do when they were waiting for the gift Jesus had promised?

2. What did Luke say the disciples did *after* the Holy Spirit came at Pentecost?

3. Which came first for the early church: prayer or action? Why is this important?

4. What was the first worship service in Europe?

5. What did Paul and Silas do when they were thrown into prison?

6. As revealed in Revelation, how does God treasure the prayers of the saints?

7. What did Samuel Chadwick mean when he said, "Prayer makes all things possible"?

Blessings Uncounted
God's Gifts for People Who Pray

If God's love to one of his people is a reason for answering his requests, if there be ten present, there is ten times the reason.

C. H. Spurgeon, "Prayer Meetings"

Kevin was a member of our church who had just returned from combat duty with the Marines in Iraq. While there, he sustained an injury to his spinal column. X-rays indicated damage to the L-5 and L-6 vertebrae, requiring surgery.

I asked Kevin if we could pray for him. Our church elders would anoint him with oil and lay hands on him in prayer as the New Testament directs (James 5:14). He consented, and we agreed to pray for him the following Sunday.

That Sunday found us outdoors celebrating our church's anniversary with a barbecue on our new property. Toward the end of the day, we gathered around Kevin and prepared to pray. It was then I realized I left the anointing oil I was going to use at home. It would have taken too long to go home and get it, but still wanting to do things "by the Book," I asked the caterer if he had any.

"No oil," he answered in a gentle Carolina drawl, "but we do have a little grease left over from the barbecue."

I hesitated while the wheels turned inside my head. *Is that okay? It's not even kosher,* I thought. But it was the closest thing at hand.

We collected the grease, gathered around Kevin, and began to pray. While we were standing there anointing Kevin, I was having a private conversation with God.

"Lord, we are messing this up. Nowhere in Scripture does it say, 'anoint the sick with hog fat.' I don't want to lack faith here, but it will *really* be a miracle if you answer this prayer!"

Puffy cumulus clouds flitted above tall pines as we bowed our heads under an attentive sky. We asked God to heal Kevin completely so that surgery would not be necessary. After the prayer was finished, we left for home.

Three weeks later I received an e-mail from Kevin, still on duty at a Marine base nearby: "I do not need surgery, and the problem with my neck and my L-5 and L-6 is gone. The doctors do not know what to make of it. Praise God!"

In worship two Sundays later, Kevin shared what had happened. He explained that shortly after we prayed for him, his pain had subsided. He went in for a second set of X-rays in preparation for surgery. The radiologist examining the X-rays found that damage to the vertebrae was no longer evident. "I feel better than new," Kevin told his befuddled doctors. "The Great Physician healed me."

Grease or no grease, God had done a miracle.

I wish that miracles like Kevin's healing happened every time we pray. But just as Paul prayed without success for his "thorn in the flesh" to be removed, there have been many times we asked for healings that didn't occur. But that shouldn't stop us from asking.

There are blessings that will come only when we pray together. We cannot dictate what those blessings will be, but our heavenly

Father calls us to come to Him. He desires to demonstrate His uncontainable love in response to our asking. Regardless of the outcome, the Bible teaches us that our prayers are always worthwhile. Jesus summed it up this way:

> Which of you fathers, if your son asks for a fish, will give him a snake instead? Or if he asks for an egg, will give him a scorpion? If you then, though you are evil, know how to give good gifts to your children, how much more will your Father in heaven give the Holy Spirit to those who ask him! (Luke 11:11–13)

God's blessings for people who pray together are too precious to miss. As Jonathan Edwards wrote, "The more excellent any benefit is which we stand in need of, the more ready God is to bestow it in answer to prayer."[1] For the remainder of this chapter, we'll consider three blessings we can't live without.

The Blessing of God's Presence

God wants us to pray so He can show us His goodness. He is looking for people who will call on Him humbly from the heart, even when they don't "have their act together." He told Israel in 2 Chronicles, "If my people, who are called by my name, will humble themselves and pray and seek my face and turn from their wicked ways, then I will hear from heaven, and I will forgive their sin and will heal their land" (7:14). God's blessings come when we repent of our sins and value His ways more than our own. Prayer and repentance go hand in hand. God waits for us to sincerely turn from our sins, and when we do, He will release His blessings into our lives.

Sometimes even the prayers of a few will start a chain reaction that will change a nation. The real power of praying together is in the inexhaustible love of God for those who are calling on Him, even if their faith and their numbers are limited. Jesus used the tiniest of seeds to illustrate that a little bit of faith can go a long way. If faith as small as a single mustard seed can move a mountain, even a few have unimaginable power when gathered together in the Father's hand (Matthew 17:20).

That's what happened at the Dutch Reformed Church in Lower Manhattan. It was September 23, 1857, and the church had been steadily declining as its membership moved to better parts of the city. Worry began to grip the nation as financial institutions fell on hard times and the fear of civil war loomed. In desperation, the church called Jeremiah Lanphier, a layman, to be a "city missionary" and to reach out to those in the surrounding neighborhood.

Lanphier's solution to the problem was to pray. He organized a prayer meeting for an hour at noon on Wednesdays and distributed fliers announcing it in the neighborhood and business area surrounding the church. The church was located a few blocks away from the Wall Street financial district, and Lanphier's hope was that businessmen would take a few minutes out of their lunch hours to pray.

When the time for the meeting came, no one showed up for the first half hour. By the time the meeting was over, only six men had gathered. But Lanphier and the few men with him didn't give up, and numbers began to increase in the weeks that followed. Within three weeks they moved out of the third-floor classroom in which they had started and into the sanctuary.[2] Other churches began to pray together as they noticed that God was blessing the meetings, and larger locations for meeting had to be found. Church historian J. Edwin Orr describes the incredible move of God that followed:

Within six months, ten thousand business men were gathering daily for prayer in New York. Within two years, a million converts were added to the American churches. No part of the nation remained untouched by fervent prayer. Not only was the population of the United States involved, but within a year or so the people of the United Kingdom—Ulster [Ireland], Scotland, Wales and England—were moved by an awakening as extensive and lasting as the Evangelical Revival of Wesley's day.[3]

The revival that followed (sometimes referred to as the Fulton Street Revival) was the beginning of the Third Great Awakening. It wasn't the result of dynamic preaching, clever marketing, or popular personalities. God's presence was released in power as His people simply called on Him and sought Him above all else. God not only blessed a church in response to the prayers of a few, He blessed a nation. Prayer meetings transformed communities throughout the country, with a profound effect on believers such as evangelist D. L. Moody (the "Billy Graham" of the nineteenth century) and William Booth, the founder of the Salvation Army.

Revivals do not happen every time a few Christians get together to pray, but God will always give a greater measure of His Spirit to those who humbly ask Him, just as Jesus promised. And where His presence is, anything is possible.

The Blessing of Unity

God's love is poured out in wonderful ways when His people join together in prayer. Love is the first fruit of the Spirit (Galatians 5:22). God longs for us to pray together because He wants to affirm His love and power among us in ways that will bring Him glory. Jesus, speaking with the Father about those who would believe in Him, said, "I have given them the glory that you gave me, that they may be one as we are one" (John 17:22). Our unity in prayer demonstrates the glory of God at work in our lives in a beautiful way.

Some of the sweetest times we can spend with other believers are on our knees. In a tender moment in the book of Acts, as Paul said farewell to the elders of the church in Ephesus, "*he knelt down with all of them and prayed. They all wept as they embraced him and kissed him*" (Acts 20:36–37, emphasis added). Samuel once told the people of Israel, whom he loved deeply, "Far be it from me that I should sin against the LORD by failing to pray for you" (1 Samuel 12:23). Paul also told the church in Thessalonica: "Night and day we pray most earnestly that we may see you again" (1 Thessalonians 3:10). One of the best ways we can express our love for others is to pray for them. Prayer is nothing less than love on its knees.

The New Testament tells us that Jesus continues to show His love for us in heaven by interceding for us daily (Romans 8:34). His example calls us to pray for each other passionately as well, if we are to be like Him.

When we hear others praying for us with spiritual insight and God-given tenderness, we can catch a glimpse of His unconditional love. Even when churches are having difficulty getting along with each other, humble, heartfelt prayer can accomplish miracles and draw us together in love. Charles Finney, one of the most influential evangelists in American history, observed:

> Nothing tends more to cement the hearts of Christians than praying together. Never do they love one another so well as when they witness the outpouring of each other's hearts in prayer. Their spirituality begets a feeling of union and confidence, highly important to the prosperity of the Church. It

is doubtful whether Christians can ever be otherwise than united, if they are in the habit of really praying together. And where they have had hard feelings and differences among themselves, these are all done away by uniting in prayer.[4]

Dietrich Bonhoeffer, the German theologian put to death in a concentration camp by the Nazis before the end of World War II, pointed out that praying with others encourages new maturity in us because it lifts us above our personal concerns and allows us to pray selflessly.[5] It pulls us up out of an unhealthy self-focus and gently restores us to our larger place in the body of Christ as we sense the needs of others and are drawn to love them through our prayers. Bonhoeffer called this an "incalculably great gift" of God's grace "for every Christian community and for every Christian."[6]

It's hard to be mad at someone when you are praying in the right spirit, mindful that the same Lord who has forgiven your sins is listening. Praying together is one of the ways that the unity Jesus prayed for naturally occurs as the Spirit convicts us, changes our hearts, and draws us together. Bonhoeffer put it this way:

> I can no longer condemn or hate a brother for whom I pray, no matter how much trouble he causes me. His face, that . . . may have been strange and intolerable to me, is transformed in intercession into the countenance of a brother for whom Christ died, the face of a forgiven sinner. This is a happy discovery for the Christian who begins to pray for others.[7]

Durham, North Carolina, the city I live in, has been marked with racial discord for generations. For several years I've met with a multiracial group of ministers who have committed to plead with

God every Tuesday morning to bring revival to our city. Though we come from a number of churches with different races and backgrounds, God has created a unity among us that is unique in our city. We've learned that when we seek God honestly together in prayer, it's impossible to remain at odds for long. The Holy Spirit begins to work on us and convict us of the sins that separate us from each other. Jesus's love softens our rough edges, and our imperfections are placed in perspective at the foot of His cross. We've found that no matter what our differences may be, Christians who "pray together, stay together." When believers join together in prayer, God's love is focused in that place in a unique and powerful way. He draws near and gently leads us to deeper places of His Spirit.[8]

The Blessing of a Growing Faith

When we pray with others, we benefit from the maturing work of the Holy Spirit in their lives. One of my first experiences of God working in this way was at a prayer meeting I attended right out of seminary. Ann Wang was a first-generation American, a Chinese believer with a contagious gratitude to God. Every time she prayed, she would begin her prayers by whispering, "Thank you, Father." With a heavy accent and fractured English, she would repeat her thanks again and again as she poured out the love in her heart for God and all He had done for her. Years later, I can still hear her voice. It was a lesson in gratitude I will never forget. She didn't know it, but Ann was teaching me how to pray in a way that would bless me for the rest of my life.

When we pray with others, we learn from their example. John Hyde was a missionary to India in the early 1900s, known also by the nickname of "Praying Hyde." Hyde had such a burden for others to know Jesus that he would spend hours a day in prayer. One of the missionaries who prayed with him wrote,

> I owe to him more than I owe to any other man, for showing me what a prayer life is, and for showing me what a *real consecrated* life is. I shall ever praise God for bringing me into contact with him . . . Jesus Christ became an ideal to me, and I had a glimpse of His prayer life, and I had a longing, which remains to this day, to be a real praying man.[9]

Praying with mature believers enables us to see Jesus at work in them and helps us want to be closer to Him. When John Wesley was traveling to Georgia as a young missionary in 1735, his ship was damaged and nearly overturned in a violent storm. A number of Moravian believers were also on the ship, and Wesley had been observing them while on the voyage. Eight years earlier, God's Spirit had moved powerfully among the Moravian community in Germany, igniting a round-the-clock prayer watch that would last for over a hundred years and lead to one of the earliest and greatest missionary movements in Protestant history.[10] As the storm raged, Wesley became convicted as the Moravians continued uninterrupted in worship and prayer. He wrote in his journal,

> The sea broke over, split the main-sail in pieces, covered the ship, and poured in between the decks, as if the great deep had already swallowed us up. A terrible screaming began among the English. The Germans calmly sang on. I asked one of them afterwards, "[Were] you not afraid?" He answered, "I thank God, no." I asked, "But were not your women and children afraid?" He replied mildly, "No; our

women and children were not afraid to die." . . . This was the most glorious day which I have hitherto seen.[11]

The Moravians' faithfulness in prayer made a huge impact on Wesley's life, and he grew deeply in spiritual maturity as a result. It's unlikely that the revival that swept England under Wesley would have happened if the Moravians had not begun to pray so fervently together a decade before. As He had done so many times before, God impacted history disproportionately through the prayers of a small group of believers.

Blessings Uncounted

When we commit ourselves to praying together, God pours out blessings in ways we never imagined. Blessings always follow united prayer. They may not be the blessings we first had in mind when we began to pray, but they will be uniquely and purposefully selected by God, who in all things "works for the good of those who love him, who have been called according to his purpose" (Romans 8:28). Monica prayed passionately that her unbelieving son Augustine would not leave North Africa for Rome, but once he did, he met the Lord there and became one of the most influential Christians in history. We may meet to pray to revive a church (as Jeremiah Lanphier intended) and find that God revives a nation instead! C. H. Spurgeon wrote, "If the Lord does not pay in silver, He will pay in gold. And if He does not pay in gold, He will pay in diamonds."[12] God will give the wisest gift in response to our prayers, pouring out His power through the generous hand of His omnipotent love. Our prayers together are the means He chooses for His hand to be moved.

Prayer Confidence Builder #5

Listening is another important part of learning how to feel comfortable praying with others. Schedule another time to pray on your own, and pray aloud just as you did in Prayer Confidence Builder #2. But this time, also take time to be silent and listen before God. Alternate praying aloud and quieting yourself before Him, practicing simply being in His presence and saying nothing.

Questions for Reflection or Discussion

1. Why does our heavenly Father want us to pray, according to Jesus in Luke 11:11–13?

2. How many people did the "prayer meeting revival," begun by Jeremiah Lanphier, begin with? What happened as a result?

3. What is the first fruit of the Spirit? How does it evidence itself when we pray together?

4. What did both Charles Finney and Dietrich Bonhoeffer feel was a key to uniting church members who were at odds with each other? Why?

5. How does the spiritual maturity of other believers benefit us when we pray together?

6. What lesson did John Wesley learn from the Moravians while traveling to America? How did praying together help them have peace in the middle of a violent storm?

7. What are the three gifts God gives to those who truly pray together?

6

The Practicality of Prayer
Giving Prayer New Priority

*It turns ordinary mortals into men of power . . . It brings
fire. It brings rain. It brings life. It brings God. There is no
power like that of prevailing prayer.*

Samuel Chadwick, *The Path of Prayer*

His name was Floyd King, but we called him "The Wizard of Ahs."

It wasn't a nice name, and he didn't deserve it.

Pastor King had come out of retirement to shepherd a little church in the sleepy desert town of Holtville, California. I was thirteen when I met him. My older brothers and I would sit in the fourth pew from the front, counting the number of times Pastor King would hesitate and say "ah" between points in his sermon. Like Joseph's brothers, we meant it for evil, but God meant it for good.

It made us pay attention. And as we watched and listened, we were able to observe a true believer in the twilight of his life. Little did I know that his impact on my life would last well beyond his years.

Not long after Pastor King's arrival, my father was hospitalized for major surgery. Pastor King would travel over twenty-five miles every day to call on Dad and to pray for him. He even took the time to give Dad a shave each morning. After that, my brothers and I dared not breathe a word about "The Wizard of Ahs." Dad wouldn't have it.

When I began to question my faith a year later, Pastor King was there again, patiently listening to my doubts. (I had a lot of them.) He and his wife quietly made themselves available, answering my questions when they could and praying for me when they couldn't. That summer I wore a path to their door and found it open, even if I hadn't called to ask if it was okay if I came by. At the end of each visit, we prayed together.

It was one summer evening as I sat on my old Schwinn ten-speed bike outside their home saying goodbye that Pastor King remarked, "We think God may be calling you to be a pastor someday." At age fourteen, being a pastor was the farthest thing from my mind. It would take me more than six years to catch up to what the Kings came to realize in the quiet moments we spent together in prayer. God, in His kindness and humor, had given "The Wizard of Ahs" a special place in my life. It wasn't courage or a brain or a heart that I found. It was a calling.

When Do You Pray, and When Do You Do Something?

Praying is one of the most practical things Christians can do together. As we seek God's presence, He gives us light for the path ahead and makes His purposes known. Spending time together in prayer is productive because God has chosen to move through our praying to accomplish things that would not have happened through any other means.

Many people struggle with spending time in prayer because they believe that God would have them *do something*. After all, James tells us that faith, if not accompanied by action, is "dead" (2:17). But

Scripture shows us in multiple places that praying *is doing something*. Yet it's hard for us to grasp that because we're culturally conditioned to equate sitting still (in this case, stillness before God) with laziness and inactivity. And that raises this practical question: When do you pray, and when do you *do something* about what you're praying for?

Our family struggled with that question in a heartrending way.

Though our daughter received Jesus when she was a small child, with adolescence came a gathering storm of rebellion and trouble at home. In spite of our best efforts, the world and the influence of friends without faith gradually took their toll. The distance between us and the daughter we dearly loved became so great that one day she simply walked away.

The urgency in my wife's voice reached through the cell phone and grabbed me by the throat. "She's *gone*," she said, choking back tears. "Katie's *gone*."

"What do you mean, gone?" I asked. "What happened? Where did she go?"

Three days earlier we had grounded Katie because we had found marijuana in her purse. We checked her purse the morning after she had snuck out of her room in the middle of the night. After we found the weed, we arranged with her high school for a stay-at-home tutor so she could finish her schooling at home. Katie had just two weeks left to finish her sophomore year.

She didn't want to wait that long.

That afternoon while Cari was on the phone in the kitchen, Katie ran away. She ran out the back door, hopped over the fence, and a moment later was running down the street. "Before I could catch her," Cari said breathlessly, "one of her friends picked her up in a car and they disappeared. In my panic I couldn't find my keys in time to follow them, and now she's *gone*." That last word, punctuated with a sob, somehow had a ring of finality about it.

"Do you know who she left with?" I asked. "Did you get a look at the car?"

"No. She had it planned out. I had hidden the phones, but she found one somehow and must have called a friend. She ran down the street out of sight and they picked her up there. It all happened so fast."

What followed was every parent's nightmare. Day after day, night after night, Katie was out on the street in our city, known for its violent crime, racial tensions, and drug abuse. We pursued every lead, but nothing led to Katie.

In the weeks that followed, we scoured the city looking for her. Police and sheriff's departments were notified, parents and friends alerted, reports filed, and Katie's name and picture circulated to law enforcement agencies throughout the state and country. Members of our church joined in the search, sending Katie's name out on prayer chains and even lending their cars so we wouldn't be recognized when we followed up tips on where she might be staying.

Nothing turned up except a couple of sightings on surveillance videos in places she was known to frequent. That gave us precious little to go on. We were always a day behind her. Out late at night and up early in the morning, we followed every clue we could find. We even thought we saw her from a distance with her friends on two occasions, only to be disappointed when we got closer.

The sleepless nights and long hours of worry took their toll. Days stretched into weeks. Like any passionate mother, Cari was so consumed with finding her daughter that she was teetering on the edge. One day, she called me from an armed drug dealer's apartment where she had gone *alone*, trying to find out anything she could about Katie. The minutes in the car as I made my way there through traffic were the longest of my life.

After that, I tried to reason with Cari and told her that we needed to be less frantic and spend more time praying, even fasting. Her response was, "I pray while I am looking."

But something didn't feel right. No matter how hard we looked or how hard we prayed *while* we were looking, it led nowhere. Exhausted, we finally began to realize that we needed to quiet ourselves and check in with God first.

Slowly, the tide began to turn. As we took more time just to pray and wait on God, our leads began to get better. People began to call us to tell us that they'd seen Katie.

By now she had been gone for over three weeks, and like Cari, I wanted to find her even if it killed me. One night I discovered she had been a passenger in a friend's car when it veered off the road and rolled over three times. The driver had been "huffing" illegal inhalants behind the wheel and passed out. Katie had cuts and bruises but ran away when the police showed up.

Another night, one of our son's friends who was helping us look for her saw her at a convenience store. She was hanging out with a girl who had been a runaway for months and a young man newly released from jail. The store clerk told us they had asked about bus tickets out of state.

For the next twenty-four hours we hardly slept. I sent fliers to every bus terminal in the area. I sat outside the bus station, watching and waiting. We did everything we could think of. Only then did we begin to realize that this was just *too much*, more than anyone can handle on their own.

The truth had finally sunk in. God alone knew exactly where she was, and He could help us find her better than anyone else.

In the end, that's how it happened. The next Sunday, difficult as it was, we took a step back from our frantic search. It was Father's Day. We spent some time with our son that afternoon and made a special effort to pray together for Katie. That evening I took Cari out to dinner in a nearby town. We heard Katie had been seen there, and we thought that we might even run into her. But when we arrived we discovered the restaurants were already closed for the day. So we headed back to Durham.

We had just pulled into the parking lot of a restaurant and were still in the car when my phone rang. It was a waitress at a diner we liked to visit just two blocks away. Katie was *there*. God had led us directly to where she was. Within two minutes, we were standing in front of her.

With a lot of love and hard work, Katie was soon on the road to recovery at home. And Cari and I discovered the difference praying together can make for those we love most of all. An English pastor from a previous generation, J. Sidlow Baxter, summed up our discovery well: "Our loved ones may spurn our appeals, reject our message, oppose our arguments, despise our persons—but they are helpless against our prayers."[1]

Walking at God's Pace: Watching and Praying

Our time in the crucible taught us a life lesson. Prayer must precede action. We must learn to wait if we want to live in a way that is effectively directed by God. Everything in human reasoning and our old sin nature will rebel against this, but we must learn how to walk at God's pace if we desire to truly hear God and discern His best for our lives. Ben Patterson describes what this tension is like in a direct but helpful way:

> For many of us, on an almost subconscious level, there is a lack of confidence that something like prayer can actually get anything done. Therefore, since our lives are full of

things that need to be done, prayer naturally gets pushed out to the edges of the day . . . God said it would be that way: "In repentance and rest is your salvation, in quietness and trust is your strength, but you would have none of it. You said, 'No, we will flee on horses.' Therefore you will flee!" (Isaiah 30:15–16). Flight is a good image of the kind of activity that dominates prayerless people and churches.[2]

Walking at God's pace does not exclude action. We act on what God gives us and go no further. Watching and praying is rarely easy, especially in a crisis when we feel like we have to do *something*. It is then we do well to call to mind Jesus's words to the disciples in the garden of Gethsemane the night before He was crucified: "Watch and pray so that you will not fall into temptation. The spirit is willing, but the flesh is weak" (Matthew 26:41).

When we watch and pray, we learn to be sensitive to the Spirit and move with God's promptings. We act on what God gives us and do no more. Then we wait again. This rhythm of praying, waiting, and acting brings a new level of effectiveness to our lives, because we are staying in step with the Holy Spirit (Galatians 5:22–25). As R. Murray M'Cheyne observed, "A breathing of believing prayer may be worth many hours' hard labor."[3]

In few places was this more evident than in the life of Charles Haddon Spurgeon. Spurgeon was arguably one of the busiest pastors in history, given the weight of his workload and his personal challenges. In an era without telephones and computers, he pastored a church of over five thousand members, directed a popular Bible school, and oversaw multiple church planting efforts and even an orphanage. He suffered at times from bouts of depression and in his later years was frequently bedridden with gout and arthritis.

Spurgeon gives this practical explanation of what the rhythm of prayer and action look like in the Christian's day-to-day life:

> We shall not fly into a passion with the Lord, and refuse to believe Him any more, neither shall we run off to novelties, and fall into the fads and crazes of the day, to try this and to try that, because God's own way is a failure; but we shall say, I have done what God bade me. I have done it in dependence upon His Spirit, and I believe good will come of it; therefore I shall wait and watch. I shall be found moving when God moves; or sitting still when the Lord tarries; but I am sure that He will not fail the soul that waits upon Him; all will be well; the blessing will come. What a sweet thing is the calm leisure of faith![4]

The "calm leisure of faith"—what a powerful thought! When we watch and pray, God is able to bring rest to the hectic pace of our lives so that even in difficult times we are lifted by His strength. This is also what Paul is describing when he writes to the Philippians, "Let your gentleness be evident to all. The Lord is near. Do not be anxious about anything, but in every situation, by prayer and petition, with thanksgiving, present your requests to God. And the peace of God, which transcends all understanding, will guard your hearts and your minds in Christ Jesus" (Philippians 4:5–7).

Why Prayer Is Action: The True Genius of Praying Together

Nehemiah provides another great example of the rhythm of prayer and action in a challenging time. While exiled with the Jewish people in Babylon, Nehemiah hears that the wall of Jerusalem is in ruins. His immediate response is to fast and pray (Nehemiah 1:4). God then gives him direction through the personal interest and response of the Persian King Artaxerxes.

All the while, Nehemiah continues to pray (Nehemiah 2:1–6). As the rebuilding begins in Jerusalem, he encounters opposition from Israel's enemies. Nehemiah immediately gathers the exiles who have returned with him. What does he want them to do together? Pray (Nehemiah 4:8–9). God then directs them to divide the people into those who will work on the wall and those who will guard the workers (Nehemiah 4:16).

There's the rhythm again: Pray. Wait. Act.

Action follows prayer.

Prayer discovers what action to take.

Prayer and action should never exclude each other. But in the busyness of the world around us, we often live that way and end up living disconnected from our real source of direction and peace. Danish philosopher and Christian Soren Kierkegaard once wrote that "the best help in all action is to pray; that is true genius; then one never goes wrong."[5] The best kind of action begins with prayer and remains prayerful throughout. As Adoniram Judson Gordon put it, "You can do more than pray *after* you have prayed; but you can never do more than pray *until* you have prayed."[6]

Prayer not only should precede action, it *is* action of the highest kind because it gives God the priority He deserves. Prayer must permeate our actions by being a continual part of them as we consciously live in God's presence. We are easily distracted, and we must fight to keep this perspective continually. It is not just a matter of "making time" for God; it is the realization that all of our time is in His hands and that we are constantly before Him wherever we are and whatever we do. This is what it means to live day by day in a relationship with

Him, and this realization helps us pray increasingly "without ceasing" (1 Thessalonians 5:17 NKJV).

Learning to give prayer higher priority takes time to grow in our lives. It rarely happens immediately because we're steeped in self-reliance. We have to unlearn old habits and patterns of thought. At the beginning of the Welsh Revival, Evan Roberts prayed with real anguish in a prayer meeting, "Oh Lord, bend me!"[7] Roberts was trained as a blacksmith, and his words painted a picture of what happens when metal is forged on an anvil. Taking more time for prayer can be like that. God works with our wills and bends us in new directions. But gently, over time, we find new peace and strength in His presence.

God desires us to be prayerful people of action: people who pray first and then act in response to His leading. All of us are at varying degrees of keeping this balance. Sometimes we tell ourselves, "I am not much of a praying person." But because *Jesus was a praying person*, you and I are intended to become like Him. Because God loves us, sooner or later He will bring us to our knees.

Jesus was also a man of action. But His action was always preceded by prayer. Prayer and action are two sides of the *same coin* of a mature and Christlike faith. You can't have one without the other. Action without prayer, even if it's done for God, too often misses the mark. E. M. Bounds describes what this looks like:

Sacred work—church activities—may so engage and absorb us as to hinder praying, and when this is the case, evil results always follow. It is better to let the work go by default than to let the praying go by neglect. Whatever affects the intensity of our praying affects the value of our work. "Too busy to pray" is not only the keynote to backsliding, but it mars even the work done. Nothing is well done without prayer for the simple reason that it leaves God out of the account. It is so easy to be seduced by the good to the neglect of the best.[8]

When actions are carried out in response to God's leading through prayer, we become His agents of light and salt in a dark and tasteless world. We are able to work effectively and with conviction because we are no longer acting on our own agenda, but with His wisdom and Spirit moving through us.

A missionary to India during the early 1900s learned this balance in a beautiful way. She had been frustrated by a lack of results in her work. She then decided that instead of asking God to bless what she was already doing, she would give prayer a new priority in her ministry. This wasn't easy at first, because she continually thought of things she "should" be doing as she started each morning on her knees. She often felt guilty, as if she wasn't working hard enough. But soon she discovered her prayer *was* work. It required special effort in a way she had never known before.

She was astounded by the transformation that followed. She wrote a friend,

> Every department of the work now is in a more prosperous condition than I have ever known it to be. The stress and strain have gone out of my life. The joy of feeling that my life is easily balanced, the life of communion on the one hand and the life of work on the other, brings constant rest and peace. I could not go back to the old life, and God grant that it may always be impossible.[9]

This is the work that changes the world. Prayer is the vehicle God uses to take us to new places of grace. When we do the work of prayer together, we willfully remove ourselves from the driver's seat. But our Father pulls us close and whispers His will to us.

He will steer us in the direction we need to go.

Prayer Confidence Builder #6

Make a special effort to join a group of people who are praying together this week. Like Evan Roberts during the Welsh Prayer Meeting Revival (see chapter 3), consider it a special opportunity to be with Jesus. As you pray, do not feel pressured to pray aloud if you're not comfortable yet. This will come in time as you become more accustomed to the group. Simply sit quietly in God's presence, "praying along" with others by silently joining them in their prayers.

Questions for Reflection or Discussion

1. Why must prayer precede action? How did James and Cari learn this lesson?

2. According to the apostle Paul (in Philippians 4), what would lead the Philippians to experience God's peace in their hearts and minds?

3. What did Nehemiah do before rebuilding the wall in Jerusalem? Why did this make his actions more effective?

4. During the Welsh Revival, when Evan Roberts prayed, "Lord, bend me!" what did he mean?

5. Where do you fall on the prayer/action continuum? Are you "more prayer" or "more action"? How do you strike the balance between both of them?

6. What did E. M. Bounds say can happen when we are too busy to pray?

At Home in Prayer

Practical Ways to Pray with Those We Love

Sanctify and prosper my domestic devotion . . . that my house may be a nursery for heaven, and my church the garden of the Lord, enriched with trees of righteousness of Thy planting, for Thy glory.

Puritan prayer

Elizabeth prayed for her little boy every day, and as soon as he was old enough, she taught him to pray with her. Neither of them knew that she had only a few more years to live. In the years they had together, they were especially close. She read the Bible to him and taught him to read by the age of four. They learned verses together and sang hymns. By the time he had reached the age of six, she had even taught him to read in Latin.

Elizabeth somehow felt that God was at work in little John's life in a powerful way. She sensed God was calling him to be a minister someday. But when John was just six, his mother died of tuberculosis. The path his life took from that day forward changed dramatically. Boarding school and then several voyages with his father, a sea captain, contributed to an increasingly unsettled and troubled life. It seemed as if the die was cast in a downward spiral, and John would be lost forever.

The story of John's adult life is better known. Forced into service in the Royal Navy, he attempted to desert and was publicly flogged. He later became a servant to slave traders and would eventually become a slave trader himself. It was during a violent storm at sea, when the ship appeared to be sinking and all would be lost, that he called out to God and found his childhood faith again. He later wrote of himself, "I, who was a willing slave of every evil, possessed with a legion of unclean spirits, have been spared, saved and changed, to stand as a monument of [God's] almighty power forever."[1]

As more time passed, he discovered for himself the calling his late mother discerned and entered the ministry. John Newton's scarred but redeemed life became a testimony to God's amazing grace, in answer to the prayers offered from a mother's loving heart.[2]

John Newton later wrote,

> Be gone unbelief, my Savior is near,
> And for my relief will surely appear:
> By prayer let me wrestle and He wilt perform,
> With Christ in the vessel I smile at the storm.[3]

The man who once cowered in fear for his life at sea now "smiled at the storm." God's faithfulness to answer a mother's prayers had continued well beyond her years, pointing her wayward son home.

When we pray for those closest to us, we leave a legacy of love. What better blessing can we give them than our prayers? In prayer, God has given us a precious gift that can impact the lives of those we love long after we are gone.

Practical Ways to Pray

For many Christians, praying with their family can be an intimidating thing to do. My father was a man of few words, and though he and Mom taught me to pray as a child, it was only in the later years of his life that I really felt at ease praying with him.

I wish I'd found the courage sooner.

Learning to pray with the people we love can be a challenge, but "we will reap a harvest if we do not give up" (Galatians 6:9).

You might have a tendency to think that your efforts to pray are weaker than anyone else's. You remember the "perfect" family who sat beside you at the restaurant while your kids were pitching a fit. You imagine them praying together with the heavenly choirs singing and the angels descending while you're wrestling with your seven-year-old's giggles and belches in that meaningful moment of silence. It's easy to think, "We'll never get this!"

But you will! God wants you to pray together, and as you keep trying He will help you learn ways of praying that will work for your personal situation. Do you remember what Jesus told His disciples about persevering in prayer? "The spirit is willing, but the flesh is weak" (Matthew 26:41; Mark 14:38). We all must work at encouraging prayer in our families; it's an aspect of family life where there is always room to grow. God is merciful and accepts our efforts no matter how steep the learning curve may be. He works with us where we are and will always make a way.

In this chapter, we'll look at natural and unforced ways to pray with those we love. First we'll take a look at down-to-earth ways to pray with children. Then we'll learn how husbands and wives can pray together in ways that are easy to schedule, are affectionate, and will practically and powerfully bless their marriage.

Let's Get Real

Jesus said that "a prophet is not without honor except in his own town, among his relatives and in his own home" (Mark 6:4). Any parents who have tried to sit down and pray with their teenagers can relate to those words! Our faults are right out there for all to see, and there never seems to be the right time to do it. But praying with our families is always worth the effort because it "brings home" the power and presence of God.

The easiest way to begin is to quietly ease prayer into existing routines. When are you sitting quietly together for a moment during the day? For married couples, this might be in bed at the beginning or end of the day. For families, it may be around the table. Think about the natural rhythms of your life together and ask God to show you those times where you can gently introduce a few moments to pray.

Our family found using a short promise from the Bible helpful for getting our prayer time started. We kept a book of Bible verse promises and a daily "flip" calendar with verses beside the table. After thanking God for our food, we'd pray briefly about whatever promise we chose for the day. Other times we would wait until the end of the meal and then share the verse and pray about whatever we had talked about over dinner. Instead of making it routine, we'd change our approach, mix it up, and try to keep it interesting.

The table is a natural place for growing together in prayer. Many families are already in the habit of praying together at mealtime. It's not a big step from "Johnny, would you ask the blessing?" to "Johnny, would you pray for Aunt Sally too? She has to go to the doctor tomorrow."

Many families say a memorized prayer at bedtime when their children are little. As kids grow, you can add a few moments to thank God for something that happened during the day or to check in about what is happening the next day (followed by a few moments to pray about it).

Keeping a family prayer journal is another great way to involve children as they grow. Using a family prayer journal not only shows God's faithfulness to answer prayer, it gives everyone an opportunity to join in. We can learn a lot from our kids when we pray. Jesus praised God because He hid things from "the wise and learned, and revealed them to little children" (Luke 10:21). Watch for God to do something special! Be sure to encourage children to pray aloud for the requests they mention as well as praying for them yourself, but don't force them to pray aloud or "preach" to them when you pray. Let them pray in their own words, whether it takes a few seconds or a few minutes. Encourage, encourage, encourage . . . and they'll look forward to it!

Any notebook will do for a family prayer journal. Write down what you prayed about and then leave room to write down the answer later. This makes for a great teaching tool. As you write down the answers God gives, you can take time to thank and praise Him for what He's done. Prayers that take longer to answer give you a chance to talk about God's perfect wisdom and how He always answers prayer, even if He says no or wait. But keep teaching moments brief so that shorter attention spans are able to keep up. Likewise, our own prayers with children should be frequent, but not lengthy. If children are taught to see prayer as an exciting and special meeting time with God, they'll be drawn to it with a sense of excitement and anticipation.

Growing Close

In a society where families spend less time together then ever before, learning how to pray together helps you stay closer. The time doesn't have to be long—even three minutes can make a difference and bring blessings that never would have occurred otherwise.

Praying together spontaneously is part of God's design for family life. God tells us to "impress" His Word upon our children "when you sit at home and when you walk along the road, when you lie down and when you get up" (Deuteronomy 6:7). Prayer shouldn't be only at set times; it should be part of the natural flow of the day. The less rehearsed and more frequent prayer is, the easier it will be to sustain. By weaving God's promises and prayer into the day, we please Him and walk closer with Him.

Home Security

Paul advised the early Christians in Ephesus to make "the most of every opportunity, because the days are evil" (Ephesians 5:16). The spiritual challenges families face today require parents to be more proactive than ever. Christian David, one of the early participants in the Moravian prayer movement, pointed out that "the enemy is always active and hard at work. The children of God must therefore call each other regularly to watch and pray."[4] Because the devil does not sleep, our homes need the security system of God's watchful power to answer prayer.

We make "the most of every opportunity" with our children by keeping in step with the Spirit and by staying in prayer ourselves. Let your children "catch" you praying on your own. Pray with them when you hear a siren (for the people who need help and for the people helping them). Pray when you drive by your church or a homeless person or an accident. When your children are afraid, pray with them about whatever their concern may be. When they are happy, point to God and use it as a chance to thank and praise Him. When someone in the family is sick, pray for healing together. Be bold and be creative, and trust God to meet you as you step forward in faith.

As Samuel was to Hannah (see 1 Samuel 1), our children are a trust from God, given to us for a special purpose. Martin Luther understood this well: "The best thing in married life," he said, "for the sake of which everything ought to be suffered and done, is the fact that God gives children and commands us to bring them up to serve Him. To do this is the noblest and most precious work on earth, because nothing may be done which pleases God more than saving souls."[5] Our children are more God's than they are ours, and our prayers with them point them to their lasting home.

Praying with Your Spouse

Praying together was one of the main priorities of married life in the New Testament. Peter wanted husbands to treat their wives with respect, "so that nothing will hinder your prayers" (1 Peter 3:7). Paul told husbands and wives in Corinth that they could abstain briefly from physical affection to "devote yourselves to prayer" (1 Corinthians 7:5). Scripture makes it clear that when both are believers, husbands and wives should share the blessing and responsibility of praying together.

Praying together *is* a blessing. Cheri Fuller writes, "Prayer will bring God's power to your house! Whatever your age or stage of life, praying together as a couple is a powerful, little-known secret to lifelong happiness in marriage. It will help keep your marriage alive and well—even rekindle your love if the flame has died. Praying as a couple is a doorway to intimacy."[6]

When we pray together, we welcome Jesus's presence and peace into our married lives. As we spend time with Him, He enables us to love each other through His Spirit in ways that we cannot in our own strength. Where He is, hearts are changed and homes are blessed.

Finding Time

How we spend time in prayer together is not as important as simply doing it. Doing it isn't as difficult as we're sometimes tempted to think. Even a few moments spent before God in prayer can make a huge difference in crucial aspects of our lives.

We considered the normal routines of our lives to find time to pray with children, and the same applies to couples praying together. When are you naturally together? Is it in the evening when you go to bed, or in the morning when you first wake up? If prayer is something waiting to be *scheduled,* it may not happen. But if it's built into a routine that always occurs, it will soon become a regular part of your life.

For couples who have never tried praying together, it may be helpful to begin by praying silently. One partner is usually more vocal than another, and this helps keep balance and make it less intimidating if either is uncomfortable praying aloud. First mention what you would like to pray about. Then hold hands, close your eyes, and pray. When you've finished praying, squeeze your spouse's hand to let him or her know you're finished. Praying this way is so easy, it can happen anywhere: in a crowded restaurant, a hospital waiting room, or in bed first thing in the morning or at the end of the day.

Praying together helps with communication in marriage, even when words are not said. When you pray, God is at work in both of you, communicating on a deeper level than words could ever reach. Simply sitting together quietly in His presence can open the door to miracles. God wants our marriages to be blessed and waits to move powerfully in our lives when we pray together.

Another great way for couples to begin to pray together is to simply thank God for each other. Take turns thanking God for the things you love about each other. You may be surprised to hear what your husband or wife is thankful for! Sometimes it's easier to say things to God about our spouse than it is to say them directly. God gives us the words as His love flows through us and into each other because we are already "one flesh."[7]

After you have thanked God for each other, ask Him to bless your spouse and then intercede for each other. Some of the most tender moments a husband and wife can share together are in prayer. This is especially true when you pray for each other's heartfelt needs. When you hear someone who knows you intimately and loves you dearly interceding for a special need in your life, you cannot help being moved.

God will pour fresh grace into your relationship with Him and with each other as you make time to pray together. Be creative! Try praying for each other at a set time every day when you are apart or arranging a "prayer date" in a place that is meaningful to both of you. Make a commitment to grow in prayer together, and ask God to show you how. Praying together protects marriages because it grounds them in power and the Word of God. The divorce rate among Christians approximates the national average of around 50 percent. But as Cheri Fuller (author of several books on family prayer) points out, Christian couples who pray together consistently not only enjoy satisfying marriages, their rate of divorce is less than 1 percent![8]

Truly amazing things await us when we reach up together in prayer. What will your blessing be? A legacy of love that reaches well beyond your years? Loved ones saved and helped by prayers that outlive you, monuments to God's almighty power? He's done it before, and He'll do it again! God's mercies, new every morning, will never fail you. He is faithful!

Prayer Confidence Builder #7

Think about your natural routines at home and where and when it would be easiest to make time for praying with your spouse or family. Then pray for God's leading, and try it this week with one of the ways suggested in this chapter.

Questions for Reflection or Discussion

1. How was God faithful to Elizabeth Newton's prayers?

2. What is the most challenging thing for you about praying with your loved ones? What would you like God to do to make this easier?

3. Have you ever used a journal to help you pray? How was it helpful?

4. What do 1 Peter 3:7 and 1 Corinthians 7:5 teach us about husbands and wives praying together in the early church?

5. How does praying together improve communication in a marriage?

6. Why do you think that the success rate for Christian marriages among couples who really pray together is so much higher than for those who do not?

The Teamwork of Prayer
Taking Time at Jesus's Feet

The one concern of the devil is to keep the saints from prayer. He fears nothing from prayerless studies, prayerless work, prayerless religion. He laughs at our toil, mocks at our wisdom, but trembles when we pray.

Samuel Chadwick

Are you a Mary or a Martha?

Most of us are a little of both. Martha loved to do things for Jesus. Mary just loved to be with Him.

Luke gives us this description of Mary and Martha in the tenth chapter of his gospel:

As Jesus and his disciples were on their way, he came to a village where a woman named Martha opened her home to him. She had a sister called Mary, who sat at the Lord's feet listening to what he said. But Martha was distracted by all the preparations that had to be made. She came to him and asked, "Lord, don't you care that my sister has left me to do the work by myself? Tell her to help me!"

"Martha, Martha," the Lord answered, "you are worried and upset about many things, but few things are needed—or indeed only one. Mary has chosen what is better, and it will not be taken away from her" (Luke 10:38–42).

Martha was busy doing things for Jesus with the best of intentions. Guests needed to be taken care of. Dinner required preparation. Needs had to be met. But with everything she had to do, Martha lost her focus. Though she started out with Jesus in mind, once she got busy, things got out of hand. She not only began to look critically in her sister's direction, she even started scolding Jesus! No wonder He said she was "worried and upset about many things."

I wonder what would have happened if Martha had taken a break from her work and sat down for a moment. Jesus had fed over five thousand before, and Martha *knew* that. What if she had asked Him to help with the few who were gathered in her home? Jesus could have prepared a meal miraculously in a moment. That would have been a dinner to remember!

I don't want to be too hard on Martha. No one likes to do all the work while everyone else just sits around, and from Martha's point of view, that's what was happening. But she was missing something *vital.*

Mary wasn't just sitting there. She was actively *listening,* engaged in Jesus's every word. Her ears and eyes were wide open, watching and waiting for what He would do next. Mary was showing her devotion to Jesus by savoring His presence and giving Him her full attention. That's why she chose "what is better."

It's not that Martha's work didn't matter. It was done out of love for Jesus, and He understood that. Terry Teykl offers this helpful explanation: "Jesus was not saying that Martha's work was not important, nor was He condemning Martha for attending to the meal. Instead He was *commending* Mary for her choice to sit at His feet and fellowship with Him."[1] What Martha was doing was good. But what Mary chose was better.

Bringing Martha Along

If you're like me, you find yourself wrestling between being a little like Mary and a little like Martha. You know that spending time at Jesus's feet is a good thing, but you also find yourself with more than enough to do. It's then you wonder, "With so many needs in this world, is it right to just 'sit there' and pray?"

Jesus seemed to think so. That's why He said Mary chose what was "better," and it "will not be taken away from her." There's a place for extended time before Jesus. Prayer and work are never meant to be separated. As we saw in chapter 6, work done without prayer is never as effective as what's accomplished after first seeking Him from the heart.

Prayer *is* work, and no one knew that better than Jesus. He prayed so hard in the garden of Gethsemane that He sweat blood (Luke 22:44). Praying together requires commitment and effort and takes time that could be used for other things. It can be such hard work that we can easily be discouraged and give up long before we should. When you carve out time to pray with others, like Mary you decide between what is good and what is better. Sometimes that won't make the Marthas in your life very happy. The challenge is to bring Martha along.

Martha needs to see the practical side of praying together. From our salvation on, the best things in our lives begin with prayer. She needs to understand that praying together is one of the most effective things we can do because it sets God's power in motion against the obstacles we face. "Prayer moves the hand that moves the world," E. M. Bounds wrote.[2] After all, the battle we're in "is not against flesh and blood, but . . . against the powers of this dark world and against the spiritual forces of evil in the heavenly realms" (Ephesians 6:12). If we want to see real change happen, we can't do it on our own. We *have* to pray and ask God's help. Once Martha understands that, she'll pull up a chair and bow her head.

Martha's desire to get things done can make praying together exciting. When you come to God in faith expecting things to happen, something inevitably will! That's why Mary and Martha need each other. Martha needs Mary's heartfelt savoring of Jesus's presence, and Mary needs Martha's desire to make a difference.

Because Mary and Martha types coexist in churches today, the pages that follow offer suggestions about how they can pray *together*. There are ideas Martha will like because they're practical (think of it as a "cookbook" for prayer) and ideas that will appeal to Mary because they make the most of time at Jesus's feet. These concepts will help people pray together for the first time or breathe new life into existing prayer groups. There are time-tested as well as contemporary ideas for praying together in groups of all sizes as well as encouragement for how to unite your church as a whole for prayer. Let's take a look!

Even a Few

Jesus's promise that He will be present when two or three gather in His name means that even the prayers of a few have incredible potential. God does not "despise the day of small things" (Zechariah 4:6–10). Simply because a prayer group is small doesn't mean God won't do great things in response! Remember, the Third Great Awakening started with a prayer group of only six people (see chapter 5).

We are culturally conditioned to think that bigger is better. Gideon felt that way when he faced Midian, until God reminded him that the sheer numbers in his army would tempt the Israelites to give themselves credit for victory rather than God (see Judges 7:1–3). Instead of looking at how big our numbers are, we should focus our attention on God and His faithfulness to answer prayer. Even the smallest group, sincerely at prayer, is a good beginning.

Growing a Prayer Meeting: Building on a Foundation of Love

C. H. Spurgeon believed so strongly in the importance of praying together that during a long absence from the pulpit due to illness he instructed his congregation, *"above all, keep up the prayer meetings."*[3] He encouraged his congregation constantly to pray, and the prayer meetings at his church (the Metropolitan Tabernacle in London) were regularly attended by a thousand to twelve hundred people. He not only knew how to "grow" prayer meetings, he was experienced in every practical aspect of keeping them going.[4] Spurgeon offers this helpful advice to pastors who want to inspire others to pray together:

Be much in prayer yourself, and this will be more effectual than scolding your people for not praying. Set the example. Draw streams of prayer out of the really gracious people by getting them to pray whenever they come to see you, and by praying with them yourself whenever you call upon them. Not only when they are ill, but when they are well, ask them to join in prayer with you.[5]

The best way to begin a work of prayer is by praying. Encourage others to pray by loving them prayerfully. If they sense you really care for their needs, they'll be drawn to pray with you. Daniel Henderson gives this encouragement to lay people wanting to share a vision for prayer with their pastors: "You cannot coerce the pastor into a burden for prayer ministry. However, a gracious invitation to 'stop in sometime' would be fitting. As he sees the vibrancy, love and support of praying saints, he will be . . . attracted to the excitement and possibility of prayer. Honey always works better than vinegar."[6] People don't want to be pressured but cannot help being drawn in if they know you are lovingly and sincerely interceding for them. Laying guilt trips won't work.

Hesitating, Stumbling, and Starting the Orchestra

Many people aren't comfortable praying in front of others. That lack of confidence can be one of the greatest challenges to starting a prayer group or getting one to grow. Some may feel that if they can't pray "well" aloud, it's better not to say anything, or even to not show up at all.

Henry Ward Beecher, a pastor and proponent of praying together during the mid-1800s (and the brother of Harriet Beecher-Stowe, author of *Uncle Tom's Cabin*) offers this helpful insight about those who feel awkward praying aloud: "The first hesitating, stumbling, and ungrammatical prayer of a confused Christian may be worth more to the church than the best prayer of the most eloquent pastor."[7] Stumbling prayers are as precious to God as any other. People who aren't comfortable praying with others should be encouraged to know how much their prayers matter, and every effort they make should be championed. Think of your prayer group as an orchestra (remember, the word that Jesus uses for praying "in agreement" is the source of our word *symphony*—Matthew 18:19). There are many instruments with many different voices, and they all have their part to play. Each one is precious to God.

Every Voice Matters

Bruce is a member of our church who is shy to speak in front of others. His sentences are short and his words to the point. (Martha would like him—he's a practical man.) When Bruce was ordained as an elder, he found himself in a group of people who prayed regularly together. Though I knew he had a faithful prayer life, in the years I had known him I had never heard him pray aloud in front of others. To encourage him, whenever our elders would pray together, I'd gently remind them how much their prayers mattered even if they didn't "get the words right," and encouraged everyone to pray even if they only did so silently. Then I began to pray for Bruce, asking God to give him the confidence to express himself aloud in prayer. I had to wait for over a year. But the first time I heard Bruce pray, it took my breath away. His prayer was brief, but so obviously from the heart, I immediately sensed God's Spirit at work. Today, Bruce prays aloud faithfully. His sentences are still short and to the point because that's who he is. His plainspoken praying is a help to all of us and a reminder of Jesus's advice that God does not hear us because of "many words" (Matthew 6:7). It's not a matter of being "good" at praying.

A Practical Prayer Meeting from Start to Finish

Prayer that matters to God is honest and from the heart. Jesus reserved some of his strongest words for those who made a "production" of their prayers. In the pages to come, we'll walk through a simple, straightforward prayer meeting. What follows is a practical approach with ideas that can be applied to groups of any size.

Preparing the Place

Just as Jesus withdrew His disciples to a quiet place and Paul met his companions outside of Philippi to pray, the space where you meet should be as free from distractions as possible (Mark 3:7; Acts 16:13). You are entering into the Lord's presence there in a special way, and it is holy ground.

Spend time preparing your spirit before you come. If you're the first to arrive, welcome the Lord by praying over the place where you meet. Quietly confess any known sin in your life to Him, because the Bible tells us that if we cherish sin in our hearts, the Lord will not listen to our prayers (Psalm 66:18). Ask God to help you love others and be "in one accord" as you pray with them, and invite the Holy Spirit to fill you and direct you together.

Worship-Based

United prayer and worship go together. God's Word encourages us to "enter his gates with thanksgiving and his courts with praise" (Psalm 100:4), and it's always helpful to begin praying together with a time of praise. Praising God lifts our eyes from ourselves and our problems, increases our faith, and encourages us in our asking as we're reminded of all God is and does. Begin with a song or two of praise, followed by several prayers of praise. (My book *Praying the Prayers of the Bible* has all of Scripture's prayers organized according to their content so that they are easily accessible. For several examples of these prayers, please see appendix 6 in the back of this book.) It's also helpful to give others a sentence to finish as a prayer, such as "Lord, you deserve to be praised because . . ." Short prayers like this encourage as many to pray as possible, and will help set the tone for participation for the rest of the meeting. Integrating worship throughout your prayer serves as a continual reminder that you are before God's "throne of grace" (Hebrews 4:16). (For an example of the order and flow of a worship-based prayer meeting, please refer to appendix 2.)

Sometimes prayer meetings may be called to emphasize specific themes or special needs. Following the opening moments of meetings where these are communicated, people should be encouraged to enter into God's presence without delay to allow as much time for prayer as possible. Many groups limit their time and power in prayer by talking too much beforehand. Set a time limit for discussion (bringing a timer works well and gives the leader an "easy out"), or have the leader encourage others to pray their requests aloud instead of talking about them beforehand. One of the members of our church has a way of cutting to the chase. If we've talked for a while, he quietly asks, "Are we going to talk, or are we going to pray?" It's a frank reminder of why we're there!

Keeping It Simple: Teaching and Tools

Prayers should be kept brief so that everyone has the opportunity to join in. Prayer that is conversational, where all pray briefly and frequently, works well for holding attention throughout the meeting.

Throughout history, long-winded praying has been one of the greatest detractors to effective prayer meetings. John Newton, in a sermon entitled "Public Prayer," wrote, "The chief fault of some good prayers is that they are too long; not that I think we should pray by the clock and limit ourselves precisely to a certain number of minutes; but it is better of the two, that the hearers should wish the prayer had been longer, than spend half the time in wishing it was over."[8] Charles Finney observed, "Some men will spin out a long prayer in telling God who and what he is, or they exhort God to do so and so. Some pray out a whole system of divinity. Some preach, some exhort the people, till every body wishes they would stop, and God wishes so too, undoubtedly!"[9] A century later, C. H. Spurgeon advised against lengthy prayers as "the ruin of all fervency, which must be exterminated by all means, even at the expense of the personal feelings of the offender."[10]

Loving and Leading

Leadership is the best remedy. Loving, spiritually sensitive leadership is vital for effective praying together, to gently correct missteps and encourage prayer that is considerate of others and keeps the glory of God as its goal. *Because praying together is a lost art, people need to be taught how to pray together.*

Enthusiastic, practical direction from a facilitator makes a huge difference. A prayer covenant or agreement, such as the one in the back of this work (see appendix 3), can be an excellent teaching tool for ensuring everyone has the same expectations. It can be handed out by the leader at the beginning of the meeting, or the group can review a point or two each week as a way of staying on target.

A covenant with a time commitment is an excellent way to encourage people to persevere in their prayers together and stay part of the group. In 1747, Jonathan Edwards asked ministers on both sides of the Atlantic to covenant to pray for the outpouring "of the Holy Spirit which shall bring on that advancement of Christ's church and kingdom." Edwards asked for seven years, but a covenant of a month or a year can be helpful as well![11] A covenant doesn't have to cover only the duration of the commitment. It may include the time at which you pray. The prayer watch covenant entered into by the

Moravian Christians at Herrnhut in Germany was a commitment to cover every hour of the day and night and resulted in continual prayer for over a hundred years (see chapter 5).

Posting general directions for the meeting is another way for leaders to gently communicate expectations. During the Fulton Street prayer revival in New York City in 1857–58, placards were posted in churches and halls encouraging participants to not pray their politics, not to exceed five minutes in their prayers, and not to pray aloud more than twice![12] Many churches benefit from projection systems today, and helpful guidelines can be easily displayed throughout a meeting or simply handed out or placed on a poster beforehand.

These twelve contemporary guidelines borrow a few ideas from the Fulton Street Revival placards and work well for prayer meetings today (for other helpful guidelines, including these observations and others, see appendix 8):

1. Arrive on time. Jesus is waiting to meet with us!
2. Pray briefly. Short prayers help keep things moving.
3. Allow others time to pray. God is waiting to hear from them too!
4. Pray passionately. We worship a loving and powerful God!
5. Don't "preach or teach" when you pray. You're talking to God, not others.
6. Please don't complain when you pray aloud, especially about others!
7. Pray reverently. You're in the throne room of the King of Kings.
8. Pray scripturally. God loves to hear His promises prayed!
9. Be silent if you like, but know others are blessed when you pray aloud.

10. Pray loud enough so people can hear—and support you in your prayer.
11. Listen quietly and follow the leading of the Spirit.
12. Pray with faith, and expect great things from God!

Other great visual aids for praying together include Scripture verses, photos of those you're praying for (such as missionaries or members of the armed forces), special topics for prayer, and the agenda for the meeting, if you have one. (For an example of a prayer meeting design that will work for either small or large groups, please see appendix 2).

Another helpful tool for organizing meetings is prayer cards, completed before the meeting begins. These may include requests, praises, and answers to prayer from the week before. When the cards are distributed to everyone beforehand, they can help everyone have something to pray for aloud and ensure as many needs and requests are covered as possible.

Topical prayer cards, such as the Bookmark Prayer Cards available through http://prayerpointpress.com (see the resources for praying together in appendix 1), offer inspirational thoughts for prayer that can serve as helpful "spark plugs" for as much participation as possible. There are suggestions on ways to praise God, scriptural blessings to pray for children, examples of prayers for revival and repentance, prayers for pastors, prayers for the seriously ill, and much more.

Following the Leader

Nothing is more vital than listening carefully to what God is doing as you pray together. Be sensitive to the Spirit and how God is leading as you pray. A clear need or theme may emerge that's different from the agenda you set beforehand. Throw the agenda out and move in that direction as the Lord leads!

Listen attentively as others pray, and pray along with them as God directs. You may want to gently whisper encouragement (saying "yes, Lord," or a quiet "amen"). Others need to know that you support them and are praying in agreement with them. God's Spirit can minister powerfully through a simple expression of love and care.

Most of all, be open to Jesus's presence. He has promised to be there and will draw near as you watch and wait. Pray expectantly, anticipating He will answer, and "the peace of God, which transcends all understanding, will guard your hearts and your minds in Christ Jesus" (Philippians 4:7).

Finishing Well

As the meeting draws to a close, end by thanking God for His faithfulness to hear and answer prayers. People should be encouraged to leave with faith, looking forward to what God will do. A song of praise is also a great way to close a meeting simply and expectantly.

Take care to end punctually at the time you all have decided upon, unless the Lord is clearly moving in another direction and there is a shared understanding that you need to stay longer in His presence. Always graciously allow people the opportunity to leave if they need to, or they might not come back the next time you meet!

The Open Doors of Prayer

The potential of our prayers together is as limitless as God's power to answer them. In every century, moments spent before Him are rewarded and blessed.

God uses the teamwork of prayer to accomplish things that wouldn't happen by any other means. He has sovereignly elected to move through our prayers together. That's why one of the first things Jesus taught His disciples to pray for was that His kingdom would come (Matthew 6:10; Luke 11:2). William Wilberforce, who with a group of evangelical Christian friends (known as the Clapham Circle) successfully prayed and strategized for the abolition of slavery in the British Empire, eloquently expressed our deep need to call on God: "But all may be done through prayer—almighty prayer, I am ready to say—and why not? For that it is almighty is only through the gracious ordination of the God of love and truth. O then, pray, pray, pray."[13]

From prison, Paul instructed the Christians in Colosse to "pray for us . . . that God may open a door for our message" (Colossians 4:3). Through united prayer, God opens doors that would otherwise remain locked and closed. Prayer is the key He places in our hands. What if we try it together?

Prayer Confidence Builder #8

The next time you pray with others, remember not to worry about the words you use. If there's an empty chair in the room where you are praying together, it may help you to imagine that Jesus is sitting in it, as you did in Prayer Confidence Builder #2. Simply pray briefly, talking to God in a natural tone of voice as you have before. You might also remember the example of the parent at an elementary school band concert (in chapter 1). How your prayers may sound to others doesn't matter. God loves to hear you pray!

Questions for Reflection or Discussion

1. Are you a Mary or a Martha?

2. What do you think would have happened if Martha had asked Jesus to help with the meal? Why?

3. What is the best way to encourage others to pray?

4. What did Henry Ward Beecher say about those who feel awkward about praying in front of others?

5. What is one of the greatest distractions for people who pray together? What is the best remedy?

6. How can a covenant of prayer be helpful? How long did Jonathan Edwards want to covenant with others to pray for revival?

7. Why is it important to conclude a prayer meeting with encouragement to have faith?

9

Lessons Learned
from a Praying Past
Strategies for Praying Together

The beginning was small enough, but we did not despise the day of small things. We met day after day.

Jeremiah Lanphier,
on the beginnings of the 1857 Fulton Street Prayer Revival

God used D. L. Moody to win thousands to Christ throughout the United States and Britain in the nineteenth century. But if you had been there when he first visited Cambridge University in the fall of 1882, you would have felt sorry for him.

The first night Moody spoke to a packed crowd of undergraduates, they greeted his American accent with guffaws. The crowd heckled Moody's simple speech, mimicked his down-to-earth mannerisms, and poked fun at Ira Sankey, Moody's song leader. One Cambridge student, Gerald Lander, sneered, "If uneducated men will come to teach the varsity, they deserve to be snubbed."

The next day was no better. The meeting was nearly rained out, and Moody later reminisced that he felt like he had "come up against a brick wall."

But he wouldn't give up. Before meeting again that Tuesday, Moody called together a group of mothers to pray. Though the students weren't their own children, 150 mothers interceded passionately for them as if they were. Moody described the scene poignantly: "Mother after mother, amidst her tears, pleaded for the young men of the university." They finished the meeting with an assurance that God had heard their prayers and help was on the way.

What happened that evening was strikingly different from the two nights before. At Moody's invitation, fifty-two young men gave their lives to Christ. Among them was Gerald Lander. His life transformed, he later became a missionary to China.[1]

Whispered Wonders

Moody knew that praying together takes passion, perseverance, and even tears. There's nothing flashy about it. During the 1857 prayer revival that swept the nation, it was decided that no announcement would be made when a well-known person (such as D. L. Moody or George Mueller) came to lead prayer. God had moved so powerfully through this quiet approach to praying together that Jeremiah Lanphier, the leader of the movement, commented, "We avoid everything that is sensational or that gratifies curiosity . . . These new things have their day, but we expect this meeting to go on forever."[2]

God tells us in His Word, "I will not yield my glory to another" (Isaiah 42:8). No matter how many different methods we use to encourage people to pray together, at one point or another, we have to bow our heads. In our entertainment-driven age, sitting still in one place and quieting ourselves may not always be the easiest thing to do. But it is a wise and restful thing to do. To do anything else is to give our attention to something less than God.

When God showed His glory to Elijah, He was not in the wind, the earthquake, or the fire. Instead, God spoke through a gentle whisper (1 Kings 19:11–13). It's in the whisper that the real wonder begins, because it's there we meet God. When we persevere together and honor God by waiting before Him, He makes himself known.

God wants to create a hunger in us for what He alone can do. Many Christians in other parts of the world understand this truth. Oxford scholar Michael Green points out,

> This is one of the main ways in which Western Christianity is distinguished from African, Asian and Latin American expressions of faith. We rely on technology, on books, videos, organization—in a word, on making things happen. People in the two-thirds world are often deprived of these things, which is a good thing because it makes them rely on God to make things happen. Thus you find the level of faith, the commitment to prayer, and the practice of fasting infinitely more developed in these continents than in our own. It is no surprise that the Gospel is spreading much faster and deeper there than it is in the West. For God loves to answer prayer.[3]

There are few better examples of a church learning to wait on God in prayer than C. H. Spurgeon's Metropolitan Tabernacle in London during the mid-1800s. Spurgeon's church practiced prayer strategically, with united prayer permeating the life of the church at multiple levels. The ways they met together show a careful, well-planned approach, and provide an example of how planning to pray can work for families, churches, and ministries today.

A Letter from a Friend

On December 1, 1864, one of the elders of the Metropolitan Tabernacle wrote Pastor Spurgeon, suggesting a special effort to pray for the outpouring of the Holy Spirit on the church. Spurgeon loved the idea and printed the letter in the church magazine (*The Sword and Trowel*) the following month. The suggestions the elder offered to his pastor for praying together are listed below. Although the language is a little old-fashioned, the ideas are timeless and powerful, underscoring the vital importance of strategic, heartfelt prayer.[4]

That you should call a meeting of the Deacons and Elders of the Church for special prayer for their own families.

A church that is driven by prayer is served by praying leadership. Because elders and deacons bear unique responsibilities in God's church, they also are especially in need of prayer. Strengthening them through a time of united prayer for their personal needs can be a strategic move, encouraging them and protecting them from the adversary, who targets those who serve in leadership. It can be the beginning of a blessing for the entire church.

That you should call a Church meeting for special prayer for a still larger blessing on the ministry, the College, the Sunday School, the Tract Visitors, the Classes, and the other efforts to extend the knowledge of the Savior now in operation among us.

Church members were to cover in prayer every ministry supported by the church in a pointed way, and they were to ask a blessing for each of them at a prayer meeting that focused especially on their needs. This was a vital opportunity to ask for God's favor for the church and for new effectiveness in sharing the good news about Jesus.

That a general meeting of the Church should be held also for thanksgiving for the blessings we have enjoyed in the past.

Thanking God for what He has done in the past honors God, encourages us, builds our faith, and prepares our hearts to receive what He will do in the future.

That you should invite from the pulpit ALL the Members of our Church to set apart, in their own homes, one particular day (which you should name) for special prayer for the outpouring of the Holy Spirit.

Notice that there are no sign-ups for this special day of prayer for God's blessing. Everybody is expected to pray on a special day—a wonderful team effort for an entire church!

That you should invite the Deacons and Elders, and from fifty to one hundred of the Members of the Church to open their houses from seven to nine on some particular evening, for special prayer for the same object. The subjects to be attended to at these meetings, and the list of the houses, to be laid before us by yourself in a printed leaflet which should be placed in every pew in the Tabernacle.

Locations for these houses of prayer were to be printed up and made available to everyone well in advance, so that the entire congregation could attend. These prayer meetings would happen in members' homes strategically located throughout the city, making them accessible to as many members of the church as possible.

That you should set apart an evening in which yourself, with the Elders, should meet all those in your congregation who are as yet undecided, but seekers after salvation. The object of this meeting would be for special exhortation and prayer with these friends, urging them to immediate decision for Christ.

Taking the time to show special interest in the visitors to our churches can have life-changing results. Calling on them at home or meeting together for gentle and caring conversation and prayer can be a powerful way to draw them closer to Christ.

That yourself with the Elders of the Church, should meet the Students, the Sunday School Teachers, the Tract Visitors, and the several Classes, for special prayer and conference, that their labors may be made more effectual in the salvation of sinners.

The "students" referred to here were those studying at the church's Bible college. Elders were to pray with every helper in every ministry of the church, in order to make their work in sharing the gospel as effective as possible. Churches and ministries are blessed when their leadership moves away from the culture of the boardroom—where human ideas prevail—toward extended time spent seeking God's wisdom in prayer. While planning, discussion, and Robert's Rules of Order have their place, they are no substitute for God's design of prayer providing direction for ministry (see chapter 4).

> That you would draw up for our consideration as a Church, and have printed a selection of promises out of the Bible which we might plead before God on this matter, and so lead us to attend to this object with understanding, having the mind of the Holy Spirit made clear to us all.

The pastor and elders made available to all promises from God's Word to bless His people in response to their prayers, so that they could pray with new power and authority.

A Week of Prayer

That year a powerful season of prayer began at the Metropolitan Tabernacle. Not only did Spurgeon follow up on all of the elders' suggestions, he also added another: a week of prayer to kick off the New Year.

Spurgeon's church met for prayer on Monday nights and kept its Bible study time on another evening so that each was given a special priority (the church still keeps these times separate today). On this occasion, they would meet in the main sanctuary and at several other church plants that had been started by the Tabernacle.

The meetings started on Monday evening, January 2. The pastors met at 3:00 p.m. to pray, and about a hundred church officers joined them at 5:00 p.m. After they had prepared with prayer, the larger meeting started at seven. Six thousand people met that evening at the Metropolitan Tabernacle to pray together! One eyewitness said, "Fully to characterize this meeting would be impossible. No pen could express the deep-thrilling power which pervaded the assembly."[5]

The pastor and a few elders led the meeting with brief prayers as others listened and prayed "in agreement." Prayers were offered asking for God's blessing, then a special time of intercession for leaders and an extended time of confession of sin followed. After a time of prayer for revival, Spurgeon preached a brief sermon, urging the unconverted to receive Christ. Similar meetings also occurred Tuesday through Friday in other locations around London, and all of them were well attended.

The Measure of Effectiveness

The size of the church isn't what makes our prayers together effective. Even though Spurgeon's church was one of the largest of its era, he never measured its vitality by the numbers attending on a Sunday morning. He looked at the prayer meetings instead: "The prayers of the church measure its prosperity. If we restrain prayer we restrain the blessing. Our true success as churches can only be had by asking it of the Lord."[6] To Spurgeon, prayer meetings had a place of special honor in the church because effectiveness in ministry flowed from the time the members spent together before Him on their knees: "May our prayer meetings be sustained in fervor, and increased in number! *Praying is, after all, the chief matter. Praying is the end of preaching.* Preaching has its right use, and must never be neglected; but real heart devotion is worth more than anything else. *Prayer is the power which brings God's blessing down upon all our work.*"[7]

So Many Ways to Unite for Prayer

Our prayers together matter deeply to God, regardless of the size of the church we attend. God's Spirit is doing a fresh work today, helping more and more people understand how much praying together matters.

There are so many ways to pray together! There are telephone and e-mail prayer chains, virtual prayer rooms on church websites, prayer walks, neighborhood houses of prayer, solemn assemblies, all-night prayer meetings, corporate fasts, concerts of prayer, prayer partners, and prayer retreats. Some churches encourage their members to stop and pray wherever they may be and ask for God's blessing at a preset time. There are prayer teams lifting up their shepherd's personal concerns, and marketplace prayer meetings in workplaces where Christians gather. There are also prayer affinity groups and prayer support groups where there is intercession for specific, shared interests (my site, PrayersForProdigals.org, offers a place for families with prodigals to anonymously request prayer). Many churches have rooms especially designated for prayer, with request cards, books, praise CDs, and other instructional materials. Some churches insert instructions for prayer during worship into several of their bulletins, randomly inviting people to lift up aspects of the service while it is in progress. Other churches turn a part of their bulletin into a prayer guide, with a scriptural promise, practical advice for prayer during the week, and a list of needs to pray for (for an example, see appendix 7). For more information on these and other ways to pray together, please consult the resources at the back of this book.

Most of all, keep praying together, even if the group you pray with is only a handful of people. God does not "despise the day of small things" (Zechariah 4:10). Neither should we!

Prayer Confidence Builder #9

The next time someone asks you to pray for him or her, try praying with the person at that moment (whether face to face, over the phone, or even via instant messaging). Here are some gentle ways to begin: "May we pray together right now?" or, "I'd like to pray with you about this now, if that's all right with you." Then simply pray very briefly. Praying with others is a wonderful way to help them with their needs and to share God's love with them!

Questions for Reflection or Discussion

1. What did D. L. Moody do when he felt like he had "come up against a brick wall"? What happened as a result?

2. Why were nationally known leaders not announced when they came to lead prayer meetings during the 1857 prayer revival?

3. Why is it important for the leaders of our churches to join together in prayer?

4. If your church or family were to design a strategy for prayer, what might it look like?

5. How do God's promises help us pray together?

6. What did Spurgeon regard as the true measure of a church's success?

7. Why did he feel that praying together was "the chief matter"?

10

More Than We Ask or Imagine
Wrestling for a Blessing

Thou art coming to a King,
Large petitions with thee bring;
For His grace and power are such,
None can ever ask too much.

John Newton,
"Come My Soul, Thy Suit Prepare"

Once there was a king who had seven sons and seven daughters. He was a kind and wise king who loved each of his children equally. He was also immensely wealthy and provided generously for his children beyond their needs.

As they came of age, the sons and daughters of the king were sent out to accomplish their father's work. Because they loved their father, they went gladly and labored long in the land. And the kingdom was blessed.

As the children grew in their love for their father's kingdom, each of them came to have the same wish. It was a good wish that would benefit the kingdom greatly, and they were certain their father would grant it as soon as they asked. So they sent the eldest brother to make the request.

He returned, looking puzzled.

"What did Father say?" the others asked.

"He didn't say yes, and I do not know why. He simply said, 'Bring one of your sisters, and have her ask me.'"

So the eldest sister went with him, and together they sought the favor of the king.

They returned, more perplexed than ever.

"What happened?" the others asked.

"He didn't say yes," the eldest sister answered, "but he didn't say no, either. He only said, 'Bring one of your brothers, and have him ask me.'"

And so the matter repeated itself, until in time, all of the sons and daughters were standing together before the king. Each of them had asked, and each time the answer was the same.

"Father," they inquired, "don't you agree that this request is good and helpful?"

The king studied each of their faces thoughtfully and smiled kindly.

"Why don't you ask again?" he said quietly. "Ask me together."

So ask they did.

"Done!" the king commanded, and immediately the matter was carried out.

"We do not understand, Father."

The king motioned for them to come near.

"I love all of you dearly," he replied. "Make no mistake about that. Each of you has a very special place in my heart. But when I see all of you together, agreeing on what is good, my heart overflows, and the kingdom cannot contain my joy. Ask what you will, for all that I have is yours."

Loved at Our Father's Throne

Our heavenly Father deeply values our prayers together. Jesus told us that "if two of you on earth agree about anything they ask for, it will be done for them by my Father in heaven" (Matthew 18:19). Because of what Jesus has done for us, we always have access to the throne room of the Father. We can "approach God's throne of grace with confidence, so that we may receive mercy and find grace to help us in our time of need" (Hebrews 4:16). It is the greatest privilege and opportunity imaginable.

When we ask together according to our Father's will, He has promised to answer. We are to ask in Jesus's name, with His purposes at heart. Jesus said, "My Father will give you whatever you ask in my name. Until now you have not asked for anything in my name. *Ask and you will receive, and your joy will be complete*" (John 16:23–24), emphasis added).

Our Father desires for believers in every century to discover the joy of praying together. When Jesus tells the disciples to "ask," the grammatical tense of the original language implies that Jesus is not only commanding His disciples to ask *together,* He also wants them to be in the habit of asking *continually.*

No matter the time in history in which we live, God warmly receives us because of our relationship with Jesus. We are commanded to go before Him in prayer and are welcomed with love when we come humbly, as Jesus did: "In that day you will ask in my name. I am not saying that I will ask the Father on your behalf. No, the Father himself loves you because you have loved me" (John 16:26–27). When we bow together before our Father's throne, our prayers are a prelude to heaven itself. Our heavenly Father loves us, and He loves it when we pray together!

Praying Together for the Kingdom

Jesus also commands us to ask *together*. Jesus's command is in the plural ("all of you ask"), and He gave it in the moments immediately before He prayed for the unity of all believers (John 17:21). Because our unity in His Spirit is so important, God has directly linked it to His willingness to answer prayer—and even to the joy He will give us!

The kingdom moves forward on our prayers. We must never underestimate the strategic importance of uniting in prayer to accomplish God's purposes. John Piper notes that "God appoints prayer as the means of finishing a mission that He has promised will certainly be finished. Therefore we pray, not because the outcome is uncertain, but because God has promised and cannot fail. *Our prayers are the means God has appointed to do what He will most certainly do*—finish the great commission and establish His kingdom."[1] Even the smallest church or most unlikely group of believers off the beaten path of society and culture may be strategically placed to accomplish God's will and purpose in a given moment.

One of the first things Jesus taught His disciples to pray for was that the kingdom would come (Matthew 6:10; Luke 11:2). Could it be that the kingdom has tarried because God has ordained that it will only come when we pray, and we have not prayed together long or hard enough?

Billy Graham discovered, "There are three things necessary for a successful crusade. The first is prayer, the second is prayer, and the third is prayer."[2] The relationship between prayer and the kingdom's progress is solidly scriptural. Jesus instructed us to "ask the Lord of the harvest . . . to send out workers into his harvest field" (Matthew 9:38). God's Word reminds us that "our struggle is not against flesh and blood, but against the rulers, against the authorities, against the powers of this dark world and against the spiritual forces of evil in the heavenly realms" (Ephesians 6:12). It also tells us that "though we live in the world, we do not wage war as the world does. The weapons we fight with are not the weapons of the world. On the contrary, they have divine power to demolish strongholds" (2 Corinthians 10:3–4). Prayer is a strategic weapon in our arsenal.

We are in a battle of cosmic proportion, and eternal souls hang in the balance. United prayer is the most effective weapon God has given us, because through it we call down His power and blessing. Prayer precedes all other work of the kingdom in its strategic importance. As Jonathan Edwards observed, "Most of the remarkable deliverances and restorations of the church of God in the Scriptures were in answer to prayer."[3] Edwards also wrote, "Christ teaches us that it becomes His disciples to seek this above all other things, and make it the first and the last in their prayers, that every petition should be put up . . . [for] the advancement of God's kingdom and glory in the world."[4] This is at the heart of what it means to pray together in Jesus's name: We pray for the purposes He lived for, caught up in the desires of His heart. The glory of God is always the goal of our prayers. As Bryan Chapell points out, "When we perceive the greatness and goodness of our God, our prayers become not so much a seeking after God for our purposes but an offering of ourselves for *His* purposes . . . We seek to have all our prayers and all that is in them honor the name of our infinitely wise, powerful, and loving Savior, knowing that when He is most honored, we are most blessed."[5]

But You Promised!

What difference could be made in the world today if we were to ask God for what He has already promised to give? God expects us to pray and waits for us to bring His promises before Him.

God would never command us to ask for things He does not want to give us. His promises are as certain as His character, and the potential for our prayers that claim His promises is as unlimited as His power. The seed of our faith may be small, but placed in His hand its power cannot be measured. E. M. Bounds underscores how vital God's promises are for our prayers:

> God's promises cover all things which pertain to life and godliness, which relate to body and soul, which have to do with time and eternity. These promises bless the present and stretch out their benefactions to the illimitable and eternal future. Prayer holds these promises in keeping and in fruition. Promises are God's golden fruit to be plucked by the hand of prayer.[6]

What would happen if we risked more in the effort and reached a little higher, stretching to grasp the promises that are ripe for the picking?

Praying God's promises enables us to keep our focus on what matters most. We pray His Word and His purposes back to Him. We bear witness of His power to save, to protect, to provide, to bless, to heal, and to set free. We pray that way not because God needs to be reminded of what He has promised but in order that we, like David, may "strengthen [ourselves] in the LORD," and our faith may be encouraged and refreshed (1 Samuel 30:6 NASB).

It is not impertinence to pray, "Father, you promised!" when He has commanded us to ask. If imperfect, earthly parents are moved by that request, how much more so is a perfect Father in heaven? One of the most poignant examples of this kind of prayer in the Bible is found in the story of Jacob, in the moments before he met his brother Esau after a long and bitter parting of the ways.

Jacob feared for his life and his family and had good reason to be afraid of Esau. Jacob had deceived him and stolen his birthright, and Esau held a grudge against him and planned to kill him (Genesis 27:41). But Jacob also knew that God had promised to bless him, so the night before he met Esau, he reminded the Lord of what He had promised: *"But you have said, 'I will surely make you prosper and will make your descendants like the sand of the sea, which cannot be counted'"* (Genesis 32:12, emphasis added).

Because God could be trusted, even Jacob (whose name means figuratively "he deceives") was bold enough to pray, "But *you promised,* Father!" Jacob knew that God's promises were reliable simply because God is faithful, not because God somehow owed Jacob a favor.

Later that night Jacob wrestled with the angel of the Lord. The match took its toll—he would limp for the rest of his life. But it ended with Jacob "prevailing" and saying, "I will not let you go unless you bless me" (Genesis 32:26). In response, he hears these thought-provoking words: "Your name will no longer be Jacob, but Israel, because *you have struggled with God and with humans and have overcome"* (Genesis 32:28, emphasis added).

Prevailing *Together*

How could anyone struggle with God and "overcome"? It could only happen if God allowed it. Why does God sometimes want us to struggle in our prayers? He wants us to struggle because there are lessons to be learned along the way, and He wants us to "overcome" according to His perfect wisdom. As the anonymous author of *The*

Kneeling Christian explained nearly a century ago, this kind of prayer "is certainly not persuading God to do what we want God to do. It is not bending the will of a reluctant God to do our will. It does not change His purpose, although it may release His power."[7]

When we push harder in prayer, we are learning to lay hold of God's higher purposes. When my children were younger, we used to arm wrestle frequently. Because I love my children, I would often let them "win." If I gave in too easily, they would tell me, "Come on, Daddy! Try harder!" So I "struggled" and "strained" and "exerted" myself until they threw all of their weight into it, used both arms, and finally "won." Then we all cheered together.

Struggling in prayer builds the muscles of our faith and teaches us perseverance. It is spiritual "resistance training." When answers to our prayers do not come when we think they should and we find ourselves having to pray harder than we ever have before, there's something of great worth to be gained. God tells His people, "You will seek me and find me when you seek me with all your heart" (Jeremiah 29:13). When we struggle together in prayer, it keeps us continually before the Father. It causes us to search His Word and seek the leading of His Spirit. The Spirit reveals to us how we should pray and what we should pray for, because "the Spirit searches all things, even the deep things of God" (1 Corinthians 2:10). When we struggle in prayer and prevail, God does not change His will. He drives us to a deeper recognition of His will and rejoices when we "win." Donald Bloesch explains, "We wrestle with God in order to discover the fuller scope of His will, and our success in this endeavor is therefore also God's victory. God accomplishes His purposes through the striving and pleading of His children."[8]

Adoniram Judson, the first missionary from the American colonies, observed, "God loves importunate prayer so much that He will not give us much blessing without it."[9] When we persist in bringing a matter before God, it doesn't automatically mean we aren't submitting ourselves to God's will. Jesus prayed through the night in the garden of Gethsemane and asked God to "take this cup from me," all the while saying, "yet not my will, but yours be done" (Luke 22:42; see also Matthew 26:39 and Mark 14:36). The Bible tells us, "During the days of Jesus' life on earth, he offered up prayers and petitions with fervent cries and tears to the one who could save him from death, *and he was heard because of his reverent submission*" (Hebrews 5:7, emphasis added). Often it is because we *are submitted* that we struggle and pray all the harder. We know the One who promises, and that encourages us to pray with passion and persistence. How could we do anything less?

In His Word, God encourages us to persist in our prayers. Immediately after He taught the Lord's Prayer, Jesus told the parable of a man who knocked on the door of a friend after midnight, asking for bread for his children. Because of the man's boldness, he was given what he asked for—not because he was a friend (Luke 11:5–8). Jesus also used the illustration of a persistent widow finally receiving justice from an unjust judge who had refused her several times. If an unjust judge will finally grant justice, Jesus asks, "Will not God bring about justice for his chosen ones, who cry out to him day and night? Will he keep putting them off?" (Luke 18:7). Because God loves us and calls us His friends, we have all the more reason to persist!

Paul told the church in Colossae that his helper Epaphras was "always wrestling in prayer for you" (Colossians 4:12). He also urged the church in Rome to "strive together with me in your prayers" (Romans 15:30 NASB). Faith shows itself in the struggle. As Bloesch points out, "The prayer of faith is importunate, agonizing prayer. God gives His promises without regard to our merits, but these promises must be claimed by faith."[10] Our faith and confidence is never in ourselves, but in our Father's love and character.

God himself invites us to come. He welcomes us with open arms. When we persist in reaching for God's promises, there may be lessons to be learned and growing to be done. But once the fruit is firmly in hand, we find the struggle has made it sweeter still.

More Than We Ask or Imagine

God blesses people who pray together. The Bible tells us that "without faith it is impossible to please God, because anyone who comes to him must believe that he exists and that he *rewards* those who earnestly seek him" (Hebrews 11:6, emphasis added). Praying together is always worth the effort, even if results seem to be slow in coming or are different from what we imagined when we began to ask. Prayer is never futile. "True prayer is always true power," Spurgeon observed. "You may not always get what you ask, but you shall always have your real wants supplied. When God does not answer His children according to the letter, He does so according to the Spirit."[11]

Jesus said that "the kingdom of heaven has been subjected to violence, and violent people have been raiding it" (Matthew 11:12). Passionate, expectant praying reaches for what God alone can do and prevails in His way. The poetic later stanzas of William Cowper's masterful hymn "God Moves in a Mysterious Way" reflect this truth:

> Judge not the Lord by feeble sense,
> But trust Him for His grace;
> Behind a frowning providence
> He hides a smiling face.

Blind unbelief is sure to err
And scan His work in vain;
God is His own interpreter,
And He will make it plain.

Several years ago when I was going through a particularly difficult time, a minister I greatly admired pulled me aside at a conference we were attending. He said, "I would like to ask you to pray with me. Let's covenant to pray Ephesians 3:14–21 for each other for the next thirty days." During the month that we prayed for each other, I contracted a waterborne microorganism and had to be hospitalized for several days. Things seemed to go from bad to worse. But in the hospital, my relationship with God deepened, and I was affirmed of His love in a powerful and lasting way.

When we persevere in prayer together, we discover how God truly is able to do "immeasurably *more* than all we ask or imagine, according to his power that is at work within us" (Ephesians 3:20, emphasis added). Bryan Chapell writes about three pastors in Scotland who met together faithfully to pray for revival during the 1950s. At the end of four years of fervent prayer, they had not seen a change and were disappointed.

Twenty-five years later, these same ministers hosted a conference for Bible-believing ministers who had begun to fill the pastoral ranks. About two hundred pastors came— roughly one-third of all Scottish ministers. One of the three pastors who had prayed for this increase asked for a show of hands by those who had been converted during those initial four years of prayer. A number in the room raised their hands . . . Then the conference leader asked those present that had been born during those four years to raise a hand. Most of the rest of the pastors then raised a hand. God had answered the prayer of the original three ministers in a way they could not have expected.[12]

When we pray together in Jesus's name, God's power is poured out in ways that exceed our comprehension. No wonder Jesus insisted so passionately, "My house will be called a house of prayer for all nations" (Mark 11:17). If we want to see real change in our world and true progress for the kingdom of God, we must reach for what He alone can do. Spurgeon once again is helpful: "Am I to do any great work for God? Then I must first be mighty upon my knees."[13]

Together, we are stronger than we ever could be on our own. We are not performing by our own strength but by God's, and He has promised His presence when two or more seek Him on their knees. How will He answer? What will He do? What blessings will only come from His hand if we ask?

There is only one way to find out.

Our Father is waiting. The door to the throne room is open, and we are welcomed with love and anticipation.

Why don't we ask Him?

Before Our Father's Throne

The wonder that we share
A loving hand pulls back the veil
And bids us enter there.
That hand for us is pierced
And holds our every care;
The presence of the risen Lord

Draws near to us through prayer.
What beauty, strength, and love!
What joy and health and peace!
With every blessing from above
Our hope and help increase.
Jesus is ever near
Where two or more are there;
The kingdom dawns and shadows flee
When hearts are joined in prayer.

~James Banks

Prayer Confidence Builder #10

Jesus said, "If two of you on earth agree about anything they ask for, it will be done for them by my Father in heaven" (Matthew 18:19). As you pray with others this week, work on praying "in agreement" by supporting their concerns and requests as you pray aloud. You might also try doing this by simply quietly saying "Yes, Lord" as they are praying.

Questions for Reflection or Discussion

1. Why didn't the king answer the prayers of his children individually?

2. Why is Jesus's command in John 16:23–24 to ask the Father also a command to ask together? What is the context of that command in the gospel of John?

3. What is the first thing Jesus taught the disciples to pray for? Is this a priority in your prayers as well?

4.   Why can we be assured of an answer when we pray God's promises?

5.   How did Jacob struggle with God and overcome? Does God change His will when we struggle in prayer and prevail?

6.   Why does God want us to struggle in prayer?

7.   What parables did Jesus use to teach us to persist in prayer?

8.   What did C. H. Spurgeon say is the prerequisite of doing any great work for God?

Appendix 1

Resources for Encouraging Prayer

Books and Periodicals

Banks, James. *Prayers for Prodigals.* Grand Rapids: Discovery House, 2011. Ninety days of Scripture-based prayers for the parents of prodigal children.

―――. *Prayers for Your Children.* Grand Rapids: Discovery House, 2015. Ninety days of Scripture-based prayers for parents and grandparents to pray for children of any age.

―――. *Praying the Prayers of the Bible.* Grand Rapids: Discovery House, 2013. A compilation of Scripture's prayers.

Cymbala, Jim. *Fresh Wind, Fresh Fire.* Grand Rapids: Zondervan, 1997. An inspiring story of how God used united prayer to revive a church.

Fuller, Cheri. *When Families Pray.* Colorado Springs: Multnomah Publishers, 1999. Forty devotions on prayer for families.

Henderson, Daniel. *Fresh Encounters.* Colorado Springs: NavPress, 2004. An excellent description of worship-based prayer in the local church.

————. *PRAY-zing!* Colorado Springs: NavPress, 2007. This book provides several examples of creative ways for people to pray together.

————. *Transforming Prayer.* Colorado Springs: NavPress, 2008. An excellent primer on worship-based prayer.

Kamstra, Douglas A. *The Praying Church Idea Book.* Grand Rapids: Faith Alive Christian Resources, 2001. This resource provides numerous concepts for individual and united prayer.

PrayerConnect Magazine!, P.O. Box 10667, Terra Haute, IN 47801 or online at prayerconnect.net.

Sacks, Cheryl. *The Prayer-Saturated Church.* Colorado Springs: NavPress, 2004. This book, which includes a CD of resources, offers instruction for helping a church become a house of prayer.

Teykl, Terry. *Making Room to Pray.* Muncie, IN: Prayer Point Press, 1993. How to start and maintain a prayer room in your church.

————. *Praying Grace.* Muncie, IN: Prayer Point Press, 2002. A training guide for praying with others for salvation, healing, and more.

————. *The Presence Based Church.* Muncie, IN: Prayer Point Press, 2003. An insightful look at the difference Jesus's presence makes for ministry in the church today.

VanderGriend, Alvin J. *Praying God's Heart.* Terre Haute, IN: PrayerShop Publishing, 2010. An excellent, all-around help for those needing encouragement in praying for others.

————. *The Praying Church Sourcebook.* Grand Rapids: Faith Alive Christian Resources. This work includes essays on prayer, strategies for praying churches, and stories of praying Christians.

Websites for Praying Together

24-7prayer.com: A worldwide effort to connect Christians in round-the-clock prayer.

cherifuller.com/FamiliesPrayUSA: Author Cheri Fuller's effort to encourage families in prayer.

dhp.org: Discovery House's website, with several excellent books on prayer.

harvestprayer.com: A site providing biblical and practical help for congregations desiring to become "houses of prayer."

JamesBanks.org: James's personal site, with blogs and podcasts encouraging prayer.

lostartofprayer.com: A website dedicated to promoting sound and scriptural ways to pray together.

momsintouch.org: An interdenominational prayer ministry encouraging moms to meet one hour a week to pray for their children and the schools they attend.

nationalprayer.org: The site of the National Prayer Committee and a resource for the National Day of Prayer.

prayerleader.com: A website devoted to growing prayer in the local church.

PrayersForProdigals.org: James's site dedicated to helping parents of prodigals pray. This site offers the opportunity for anonymous prayer requests.

Prayforrenewal.org: A site assisting pastors and local churches in furthering individual and united prayer and the development of church prayer rooms.

DVDs and Other Resources

Banks, James. *Praying with Jesus.* Grand Rapids: Discovery House, 2016. This DVD and study guide set looks at Jesus's teaching and personal practice of prayer, including encouragement to pray with others.

Cymbala, Jim. *When God's People Pray.* Grand Rapids: Zondervan, 2012. An instructive, six-session DVD on the importance of prayer and praying together.

My House, a House of Prayer. This is a sermon given at the 1994 Praise Gathering in Indianapolis, Indiana, on the vital need for united prayer in the contemporary church. It can be purchased at the website store of Life Action Revival Ministries: lifeaction.org /store/category/dvd/.

Orr, J. Edwin. *The Role of Prayer in Spiritual Awakening.* This is a DVD about the importance of united prayer for revival through-out history.

Prayer Cards. A variety of Scripture-based cards designed to encourage individual or group prayer are available for download at no cost at prayforrenewal.org (Go to the "Resources" section and click on "Prayer Guides.") Others may be purchased in quantity online at navpress.com/pray. (Click on "Corporate Prayer.")

Appendix 2

A Worship-Based Prayer Meeting

The purpose of a worship-based prayer meeting is to encourage as much time in the Lord's presence as possible. A prayer meeting is an appointment with God. The goal of this meeting is spending time at Jesus's feet and persevering in fervent prayer together. The basic outline below provides flexibility for small or large groups. This approach encourages the group leader to either begin with prayer or go straight to prayer as quickly as possible. The meeting is designed to last for an hour but can be done in less time for a lunchtime or marketplace prayer meeting.

Beginning

Be there early and be in quiet prayer as others gather. This will serve as a reminder that you are in a holy place, and will help keep conversation to a minimum. Before the meeting begins, set the atmosphere with soft keyboard or guitar music. Then, as the meeting begins, the leader welcomes others with just a few sentences and encourages them to quiet their hearts before the Lord.

A Moment of Silence

Those gathered spend a moment before the Lord privately confessing any sin and entering lovingly and reverently into His presence. They invite the Holy Spirit to lead the group and to help them to pray. Just one minute of silence can be surprisingly effective.

Praying Together: Three Components

Entering God's Gates

Effective prayer starts with heartfelt worship because it encourages faith in our matchless God. It's helpful to begin with a song or two of praise. The leader begins energetically, with a brief prayer of praise from Scripture (please see appendix 6 for examples). Encourage others to spend several minutes simply adoring God, *before a single request is made.* You might also ask others to search their Bibles for verses of praise to pray aloud. Daniel Henderson, who has written several helpful books on worship-based prayer, encourages participation by giving others a simple sentence to finish, such as "Lord, I love you because . . ." or "You are wonderful because . . ."

Bowing before His Throne

Be sensitive to the Holy Spirit about when to begin praying for others. (Sometimes the entire meeting may be spent in praise; at other times you may move more quickly into urgent needs or be led into a time of listening and silence.) Requests are best shared by simply praying about them. This maximizes time in prayer, enabling you to go straight to the One who can do something about the need. By addressing God, you inform everyone present of the needs at hand while removing the temptation to gossip. God knows each need, so the actual description of circumstances should be brief. Needs may also be shared by distributing prayer request cards for individuals to pray aloud (screen them for confidentiality purposes beforehand). The cards may be collected earlier during a worship service or filled out as the meeting begins. The leader may also help maintain momentum by asking those who feel comfortable praying before others to lift up particular needs aloud. This may be done by asking others by name or by simply asking, "Would someone please pray for . . . ?"

For groups larger than twenty, it's helpful to break up into pairs or threes when praying for requests. Allow people two to three minutes to get into groups and share their requests conversationally among themselves before praying together. A gentle reminder that "you should begin praying now" after three minutes is helpful. Requests requiring the prayer of all may be briefly shared by the leader while people are clustered in small groups.

In groups of all sizes, be sure to encourage agreement in prayer while others are praying aloud. Praying for a need more than once or joining in with a gentle "Yes, Lord" or "Please, Father" lets others know that their needs are being heard with love.

Looking Forward in Faith

Express confidence in God's ability to answer prayer. The importance of emphasizing God's faithfulness cannot be overstated. Thank God that He hears your prayers and will answer with perfect wisdom. Thank Him in advance for the answers that will come to your prayers. Matthew 13:58 tells us that Jesus did not do many miracles in His hometown "because of their lack of faith." Prayer meetings that end without faith will see little or nothing happen as a result of praying. Pray expectantly, and quote God's promises in Scripture for the needs at hand.

Conclude the meeting with a brief prayer of thanks or with a simple worship chorus that is also a prayer. The leader may also read a brief, uplifting verse, encouraging all to look forward to what God will do.

Appendix 3

A Covenant for Praying Together

I covenant to pray with other Christians out of obedience to Jesus's command and example (Matthew 6:9; 9:38; 18:19–20; Luke 9:29). I recognize there are blessings God will give only if we join together in prayer (John 16:23–24).

I will endeavor to be supportive and encouraging to others as we pray and to "make every effort to keep the unity of the Spirit through the bond of peace" (Ephesians 4:3). I will make an effort to pray before I arrive so that I may seek God humbly and from the heart (2 Chronicles 7:14). I will prepare myself by asking for God's forgiveness and repenting of my sins, so that my prayers may be heard (Psalm 66:18). I will be kind and compassionate to others, forgiving them just as God has forgiven me through Jesus (Ephesians 4:32).

I agree to listen as well as to pray, seeking to be sensitive to the leading of the Holy Spirit (John 10:3; Ephesians 6:18). I will not delay the meeting by talking too much (Ecclesiastes 5:2). I will be attentive to Jesus's presence, because He has promised to join us in a special way when we pray together (Matthew 18:20). I will recognize that I am in His presence, and that it is not the place for me to preach to others or instruct them while I pray (Psalm 46:10). I will address God alone with a reverent heart (Jeremiah 33:3). I will also make my spoken prayers brief so that others may have the opportunity to pray aloud and so that our time may be shared equally (1 Thessalonians 5:19). I will do my best to pray through the whole meeting, whether

I am praying aloud or praying silently (1 Thessalonians 5:17). I recognize that it is not our words that matter, but our hearts before God (Matthew 6:7).

I will do my best to arrive on time so that I will not be a distraction to others as they pray together (1 Corinthians 14:40). I will attend faithfully in order to be an encouragement to others (Hebrews 10:25). I will also be supportive of our leader's efforts to help us begin and end on time so that we can minimize time in conversation and maximize time in prayer (Isaiah 55:6; Ephesians 5:21; Hebrews 13:17).

I will keep God's glory and His kingdom a priority in my prayers, because it is the first thing Jesus taught us to ask for (Matthew 6:10; Luke 11:2; Revelation 22:20). I will seek to pray in unity and love with my brothers and sisters in Christ, so that our heavenly Father will answer our prayers (Matthew 18:19; Colossians 3:12–14). I will guard against gossip and keep private matters confidential for the good of all (Proverbs 11:13; 2 Corinthians 12:20).

I will pray in faith, believing that God answers prayer with all wisdom and has called me to know the joy of receiving answers to prayer (John 16:24; James 1:5–6). I will stand on God's promises to His people, trusting that He will keep them in His perfect way (Hebrews 10:23). I will pray for my brothers and sisters while we are apart, that we may be faithful witnesses to Jesus wherever we may be (Colossians 4:2–4). I will watch expectantly for God to move in response to our prayers and believe that He is "able to do immeasurably more than all we ask or imagine, according to his power that is at work within us, to him be glory in the church and in Christ Jesus throughout all generations, for ever and ever! Amen" (Ephesians 3:20–21).

Signature _____**Date** _____

Appendix 4

Getting Started

Six Exercises to Help You Learn How to Pray as a Group

It takes time to learn how to pray together. Many groups begin with the best of intentions but find after a few meetings that attendance dwindles and enthusiasm wanes.

Why is that? Often, it's because we simply don't know *how* to pray together well. Our adversary also loves to throw any stumbling blocks in our path because he fears the power that our prayer releases. As hymn writer William Cowper pointed out, "Satan trembles when he sees the weakest saint upon their knees."

Praying together requires commitment. We need to see it more as a marathon than a sprint and pace ourselves to go the distance.

It is also a work in progress. We get better at it over time. Once we learn a few basic principles, it's much easier to stay the course.

If you're wondering how your group can grow strong in prayer, here's help! The following pages are designed to provide some basic principles and a solid foundation for any group. You'll find six exercises that can easily be used to start a new prayer group or breathe life into an existing one. They can be used over a period of days or weeks. We also recommend that you use the prayer covenant in appendix 3 of *Praying Together* as a way of communicating up front your expectations for the group and the length of your commitment to pray.

May God bless you (and many others) as you pray!

Help 1: Beginning on Time

Let us then approach God's throne of grace with confidence, so that we may receive mercy and find grace to help us in our time of need.

Hebrews 4:16

Goal: More prayer, less talk.

When we pray together, we enjoy an incredible privilege. God *wants* us to pray and to enter into His presence. We are invited and welcome!

One of the greatest challenges for people who pray together is that of simply getting started. It's easy to spend a lot of time discussing what to pray about instead of actually praying. One member of the church I serve puts it rather bluntly when our conversation goes a little long: "Are we going to pray, or are we going to talk?"

He's right. There's nothing wrong with discussing needs, but there should also be a shared understanding that the main reason we are meeting together is to seek God. He is the greatest source of help and comfort for every matter we discuss.

Today, we will limit our conversation of what to pray about to five minutes. We'd like to ask everyone's help to begin praying together on time. (If someone would like to be a timekeeper, please volunteer!) Our goal is to maximize prayer and the time we spend before God. This is also one of the best ways we can love one another, because we're taking our needs straight to the Father.

If there isn't enough time to share your concern, simply bring it up as a prayer.

As you talk to God about your concern, others will make an effort to support you and join in.

Let's get started! God is waiting, and so are the blessings that He alone can give.

Help 2: Sharing the Time

And when you pray, do not keep on babbling like pagans, for they think they will be heard because of their many words.

Matthew 6:7

Goal: To encourage as many to pray aloud as possible.

Materials: Two pennies for every participant and a small basket.

It's easier for some folks to talk than others. But when we pray together, it's not the number of words we use that matter. If words don't come easily for you, you may feel you're not very good at praying. But the sentences we string together have little to do with it.

The Bible tells us, "People look at the outward appearance, but the LORD looks at the heart" (1 Samuel 16:7). God's Word also says, "Do not be hasty in your heart to utter anything before God," and even tells us to let our words "be few" (Ecclesiastes 5:2). A few words spoken from a heart intent on loving God can be "powerful and effective" (James 5:16).

Today we'd like to encourage everyone to pray aloud. We'd also like to ask everyone to keep their prayers brief. Even if you pray only a sentence or two, don't worry about what others think. You are talking to God, not others. To give everyone a chance to pray, we're going to give everyone two pennies. Each time you pray, put your penny in the basket in the center of the group. When you've prayed your "two cents' worth," you can pray silently as others pray aloud. Let's pray!

Help 3: Simply Talking to God

The Pharisee stood by himself and prayed: "God, I thank you that I am not like other men—robbers, evildoers, adulterers—or even like this tax collector. I fast twice a week and give a tenth of all I get."

> *But the tax collector stood at a distance. He would not even look up to heaven, but beat his breast and said, "God, have mercy on me, a sinner."*
>
> *I tell you that this man, rather than the other, went home justified before God. For all those who exalt themselves will be humbled, and those who humble themselves will be exalted.*
>
> Luke 18:11–14

Goal: To encourage prayer that is uplifting and spoken directly to God.

Do you know what a "Your Mama" prayer is? It's the kind of prayer your mother prays when you're little and she knows you're listening: "Help Johnny to take out the trash every night, eat his peas, and to always do what Mommy says . . ."

Sometimes it's tempting to talk to others when we pray. The Pharisee Jesus mentions is doing that. He isn't really praying. He's drawing attention to himself, and as a result his prayer isn't heard. Praying and talking to others are two very different things.

We also have to be careful not to talk *about* others in inappropriate ways. Our praying together should never allow gossip, complaints, or veiled "messages" to others. In order for God to bless us when we pray, we have to pray in love (John 15:16–17).

As we pray today, just talk to God simply and humbly. James tells us to "humble yourselves before the Lord, and he will lift you up" (4:10). Peter also tells us to "humble yourselves . . . under God's mighty hand, that he may lift you up in due time" (1 Peter 5:6). Humble prayer is the most uplifting prayer of all!

Help 4: Praying More than Needs

Enter his gates with thanksgiving and his courts with praise;
give thanks to him and praise his name.

Psalm 100:4

Goal: To praise and thank God more when we pray.

In *Fresh Encounters*, Daniel Henderson explains that prayer meetings at his church begin with a Scripture reading and a discussion of who God is, not with a personal airing of concerns or requests: "I usually say, 'For the next ten minutes you cannot ask God for anything— only give Him what He deserves. If you ask for something, a trap door will open under your seat'" (p. 137).

Of course there are no "trap doors" at Henderson's church, but his point is well taken. How often do we rush into God's presence with our problems instead of first thanking and praising Him?

Psalm 100 describes a gradual drawing near to God's presence in the temple through thanks and praise. Worshiping God lifts us above our own limitations and opens our minds and hearts to His all-sufficient grace. As we begin to recognize who God is, we are better able to seek His heart as we pray.

As we pray together today, let's begin by simply enjoying God's presence. We'll thank and praise Him for the first ten minutes without offering any requests. (Remember that trap door!) God is always worthy of our worship. Let's give it to Him!

Help 5: Learning How to Listen

I will listen to what God the LORD says; he promises peace to
his people, his faithful servants—but let them not turn to folly.

Psalm 85:8

Goal: To become more comfortable with silence when praying together.

Are you a Mary or a Martha?

Mary was comfortable just being at Jesus's feet. Martha felt like she had to do *something.*

When many begin to pray together, they feel like Martha. They're uncomfortable with what seems to be just "sitting there," and they say something (anything!) to fill the silence. But Mary was doing much more than sitting. She was actively listening and enjoying Jesus's presence.

Today as we pray together, we'll practice spending time in silence before the Lord. After we've prayed for ten minutes, we'll spend another five in silence. This may take some focus and self-discipline because we are culturally inclined to being entertained (and have shorter attention spans as a result).

God's Word reminds us, "In repentance and rest is your salvation, in quietness and trust is your strength" (Isaiah 30:15). As we're quiet before the Lord, He draws near and helps us to pray by prompting our hearts and minds through His Spirit. Let's begin this time by asking Him to direct us, and then pray as He leads us.

Help 6: Praying in Step

Since we live by the Spirit, let us keep in step with the Spirit.
Galatians 5:25

Goal: To pray in unity with God's desires.

Jesus taught us to pray for God's kingdom above all other things. It's the first request of the Lord's Prayer. Our Father wants us to "seek *first* his kingdom and his righteousness," and makes it clear that as we do, our own needs will be met (Matthew 6:33, emphasis added).

Praying for God's purposes helps us to honor Him. When we set our personal agendas aside, we humble ourselves and pray with servants' hearts. We also pray strategically, because we are asking for things that God has said in His Word He desires to happen. God has made His purpose clear. He wants His kingdom to come and waits for us to ask for it. He wants the lost to be found, because Jesus came "to seek and to save the lost" (Luke 19:10). These are prayers He loves to answer!

Jesus also wants us to pray with unity: "Again, truly I tell you that if two of you on earth agree about anything they ask for, it will be done for them by my Father in heaven" (Matthew 18:19). As we pray together today, let's make our requests with God's desires at heart. As you hear someone pray for God's purposes, join them in their request when you pray aloud. Let's also support each other with gentle verbal encouragement and offer an occasional "yes, Lord" or "amen" to show our agreement with others when they pray.

Our Father is waiting. Let's go to Him now. Let's pray *together!*

Appendix 5

Composing a Concert of Prayer

A concert of prayer is (by definition) a "concerted prayer effort." It is sometimes compared to a symphony in the sense that it is able to bring many voices together to pray in unison and has many parts. The following is an example of a simple outline, or "composition," for a concert of prayer:

Prelude

1. Welcome.
2. Scriptural precedents for praying together.
3. Joining together in small groups for prayer.

First Movement

1. Confessing our sin and humbling ourselves before God.
2. Professing our inadequacy and God's complete sufficiency.
3. Inviting God's Spirit to fill, lead, and direct our prayer together.

Second Movement

1. Intercession for particular needs or a stated purpose.
2. Listening before God and quieting ourselves in His presence.
3. Praying about matters God has brought to mind.

Third Movement

1. Prayer for unity in the body of Christ.
2. Prayer for the harvest and evangelization of our nation and world.
3. Prayer for the kingdom to come.

Finale

1. Prayer for power to live as God's faithful and obedient servants.
2. Prayers of faith in God's ability to answer prayer and thanks for what He will do as a direct result of our praying together.
3. Prayers of praise.

Appendix 6

Scriptural Prayers of Praise

These brief examples of prayers of praise are adapted from *Praying the Prayers of the Bible* (by James Banks, Discovery House, 2011), a comprehensive collection of Scripture's prayers organized according to their contents (there are several other categories of prayer in God's Word). There is no better teaching tool for prayer than the prayers of the Bible.

You alone are God

May your glorious name be praised! May it be exalted above all blessing and praise! You alone are the LORD. You made the skies and the heavens and all the stars. You made the earth and the seas and everything in them. You preserve them all, and the angels of heaven worship you.

From Nehemiah 9:5–6

I will praise you with all of my heart

I will praise you, LORD, with all my heart; I will tell of all the marvelous things you have done. I will be filled with joy because of you. I will sing praises to your name, O Most High.

Psalm 9:1–2

You are the fountain of life!

Your unfailing love, O LORD, is as vast as the heavens; your faithfulness reaches beyond the clouds. Your righteousness is like the mighty mountains, your justice like the ocean depths. You care for people and animals alike, O LORD. How precious is your unfailing love, O God! All humanity finds shelter in the shadow of your wings. You feed them from the abundance of your own house, letting them drink from your river of delights. For you are the fountain of life, the light by which we see.

Psalm 36:5–9

Each morning I will sing to you

As for me, I will sing about your power. Each morning I will sing with joy about your unfailing love. For you have been my refuge, a place of safety when I am in distress. O my Strength, to you I sing praises, for you, O God, are my refuge, the God who shows me unfailing love.

Psalm 59:16–17

You carry us in your arms

Praise the Lord; praise God our savior! For each day you carry us in your arms.

Psalm 68:19

Praise God for the Son of David!

Praise God for the Son of David! Blessings on the one who comes in the name of the LORD! Praise God in highest heaven!

from Matthew 21:9

Worthy is the Lamb who was slaughtered

You are worthy to take the scroll and break its seals and open it. For you were slaughtered, and your blood has ransomed people for God from every tribe and language and people and nation. And you have caused them to become a Kingdom of priests for our God. And they will reign on the earth. Worthy is the Lamb who was slaughtered—to receive power and riches and wisdom and strength and honor and glory and blessing.

from Revelation 5:9–10, 12

Appendix 7

A Church Bulletin Prayer Help

The following is an example of a church bulletin page or insert designed to help members grow in their practice of prayer during the week, uniting in prayer for the same goals. It includes a prayer promise (which is new every week), a monthly goal to pray for, scriptural prayer guidelines (which may be based on the sermon), a practical prayer suggestion, and a list of prayer needs from the congregation.

Help with Prayer

Prayer Promise for the Week:

"Can a mother forget the baby at her breast and have no compassion on the child she has borne? Though she may forget, I will not forget you!" [declares the Lord].

Isaiah 49:15 (NIV)

Monthly Prayer Focus:

To know the joy of serving our Father above ourselves.

Practicing Prayer This Week:

1. Moses's response to God (in our Scripture this week) was mistaken because he looked first at himself and his abilities. Do you ever limit what God could do through you like this?
2. Augustine said, "Our hearts are restless until they find rest in Thee." Spend some time resting in God and thanking Him for being able to do all things.
3. Serving God is often challenging, but it's ultimately eternally more rewarding than serving ourselves. Ask God to give you grace to serve and love Him above all.
4. Sing a hymn or a praise song to God as a way of loving Him. Make one up if you like, and sing from the heart!

Prayer Suggestion:

The next time someone asks you to pray about something, volunteer to pray in that moment, "on the spot!"

Others to Pray For:

Praise God for Brandon Keith, 8 lbs., 8 ounces!

Rebecca Raines—surgery on both knees

Mark Autry—stroke recovery

Brenda Wilkinson—gall bladder surgery recovery

Jennifer Carlson—T-cell lymphoma, a form of cancer in the blood

Pastor James—recovering from hernia surgery

Harold Carson—friend of Bill Williams, prostate cancer

Jennifer & Scott Johnson—praise God for the gift of a baby

Joey McAdams—safety while serving in Iraq

John Anderson—for safety during incarceration
Richard Hansen—stroke recovery and general health improvement
A. C. Wilson—for pain relief from a facial nerve condition

Appendix 8

Guidelines for Corporate Prayer

The helpful guidelines below are provided with the permission of their author, Rev. David Beaty, pastor of River Oaks Church in Clemmons, North Carolina.

Guidelines for Corporate Prayer

They all joined together constantly in prayer.

Acts 1:14

Both Scripture and history show us that there is great power in united prayer by God's people. God has repeatedly used corporate prayer meetings to prepare the way for revival. United prayer by His people is foundational to the work that God does in and through His church.

But sometimes our human faults and biases can hinder the effectiveness of a corporate prayer gathering. Unity can be broken and discouragement can set in when we are not sensitive to the needs of others with whom we pray. Prayer meetings need to be based upon biblical principles and Christian love for those praying with us.

Here are some guidelines that I think will help us have greater unity and effectiveness when praying with others:

- Don't monopolize the prayer time by praying too long. Remember, if ten people are gathered to pray for an hour, each person, on average, will have only six minutes to lead in prayer. Yet I have seen people come into a meeting and pray nonstop for fifteen minutes or more. When one person prays too long, the others tend to tune out and can become discouraged about corporate prayer.

- Try to stay with the theme for which God is directing the group to pray. If several people have prayed for leaders or ministries of the church, don't abruptly change direction by praying for a sick family member. There may be a time later in the meeting when prayer is focused on healing for the sick, and it would be more appropriate to pray for your family member then. A time of silence during a lapse in prayer often provides an appropriate time to change the focus of your prayers.

- Be willing to allow silence. Some people seem to be uncomfortable with silence in prayer meetings, and they quickly jump in any time there is quiet for several seconds. The Bible encourages us to wait in silence for God (Psalm 62:1, 5), so times of quiet are to be expected. Less assertive people and those for whom prayer is new will tend to wait for times of extended silence before praying aloud. Plus, silence allows us all time to listen for what the Lord may impress upon our hearts.

- Do not project your own discouragement onto the group. While there is a time to pour out your heart before God (Psalm 62:8), this is typically best done alone or with a friend or two who will pray for you. If you are too deeply burdened or depressed to pray with a group, ask a few people to come aside and pray just for you.

- Don't "pray a complaint." It is unfortunate, but some people use prayer meetings to air their grievances about a church or its leaders. Before praying about something in your church that frustrates you, consider how it might be heard by others. Could it reflect negatively on a leader? Could it negatively impact someone else's attitude about the church? If so, it would be best prayed about in individual, rather than corporate, prayer.

- Pray scripturally. Since all Scripture is inspired by God (2 Timothy 3:16), He will never lead us to pray for something that is contrary to biblical teaching. That's why it is important to study the Bible regularly as we grow in our understanding of prayer.

- Don't use your prayer to teach, preach, or attempt to assert your opinions upon others. Remember that you are addressing God, not people. Avoid praying in a way that you would not pray if alone with God.

- Pray in such a way that others can understand you. The gift of tongues is a valuable spiritual gift that can often be used in prayer. But in a group setting, a message in tongues must be interpreted (conveyed in a known language) in order to be of value to the hearers (1 Corinthians 14:6). The apostle Paul explained that unless there is an interpreter for the message in tongues, "the speaker should keep quiet in the church and speak to himself and to God" (1 Corinthians 14:28).

- The biblical principle for the use of all spiritual gifts is to put others first. Consider what would be edifying and encouraging to them, and put their interests above your own desires.

- Praying so that others can understand us also applies to our known language. Obviously, we should pray loudly enough for all to hear. But we should also avoid praying about issues that would be foreign to others in the group. And we should avoid using terms they would not understand.

- Lastly, always examine your heart for pride in corporate prayer meetings. Our prayers should never spring from a motive to impress others with our spirituality. Pray with humility, sincerity, and for the glory of God alone.

Notes

Chapter 1: Me? Pray with Others?

1. Matthew Henry, *Commentary on the Whole Bible*, vol. 4, Christian Classics Ethereal Library, ccel.org.
2. William Cowper, "What Various Hindrances We Meet," in *The Olney Hymns* (London: W. Oliver, 1779), no. 60.
3. C. H. Spurgeon, "The Special Prayer Meeting," in *The C. H. Spurgeon Collection* (Rio, WI: Ages Software, 1998–2001), 21:553.
4. This information is from a plaque at the Frank Morrow Graham Academic Center at Gordon-Conwell Theological Seminary in Charlotte, North Carolina.
5. Bill Hybels, *Just Walk Across the Room* (Grand Rapids, MI: Zondervan Publishing, 2006), 207.
6. Henry Blackaby and Claude V. King, *Experiencing God* (Nashville, TN: Broadman and Holman, 1994), 19.
7. George Barna, "Church Priorities for 2005 Vary Considerably," Barna Group, 14 February 2005. Web.

Chapter 2: A Closer Look at a Lost Art

1. Joyce G. Baldwin, *Esther*, vol. 12 of *Tyndale Old Testament Commentaries* (Leicester, England: Intervarsity Press, 1984), 80.
2. Exodus 2:23, 14:10; Numbers 20:16; Deuteronomy 26:7; Judges 3:9; 3:15; 6:6; 10:10.

3. C. H. Spurgeon, "Prayer Meetings," in *The C. H. Spurgeon Collection* (Rio, WI: Ages Software, 1998–2001), 60:526.

4. Jonathan Edwards, *An Humble Attempt to Promote Explicit Agreement and Visible Union of God's People in Extraordinary Prayer for the Revival of Religion and the Advancement of Christ's Kingdom on Earth*, vol. 2 of *The Works of Jonathan Edwards* (Peabody, MA: Hendrickson Publishers, 1998), 295.

Chapter 3: Where Two or More

1. Daniel Henderson, *Fresh Encounters* (Colorado Springs, CO: NavPress, 2004), 107.

2. Andrew Murray, *With Christ in the School of Prayer* (Gainesville, FL: Bridge-Logos, 1999), 115.

3. Ole Hallesby, *Prayer* (Minneapolis, MN: Augsburg Fortress, 1994), 30.

4. Henderson, 64.

5. Jim Cymbala, *Fresh Wind, Fresh Fire* (Grand Rapids, MI: Zondervan, 1997), 28.

6. Quotation from a lecture by Kevin Adams at Gordon-Conwell Theological Seminary, January 14, 2005.

7. Murray, xxiii.

Chapter 4: Catching the Wind

1. C. H. Spurgeon, "A Call to Prayer and Testimony," in *The C. H. Spurgeon Collection* (Rio, WI: Ages Software, 1998–2001), 37:123.

2. Samuel Chadwick, *The Path of Prayer* (Fort Washington, PA: CLC Publications, 2000), 18.

3. Armin Gesswein, "Jesus Builds a Prayer Meeting." Web. 28 July 2009.

4. C. H. Spurgeon, *Only a Prayer Meeting* (Geanies House, Fearn, Scotland: Christian Focus Publications, 2000), 9.

5. John Piper, *A Godward Life* (Sisters, OR: Multnomah Publishers, 1997), 234.

Chapter 5: Blessings Uncounted

1. Jonathan Edwards, *An Humble Attempt to Promote Explicit Agreement and Visible Union of God's People in Extraordinary Prayer for the Revival of Religion and the Advancement of Christ's Kingdom on Earth*, vol. 2 of *The Works of Jonathan Edwards* (Peabody, MA: Hendrickson Publishers, 1998), 290.

2. Kathryn T. Long, *The Revival of 1857–58* (New York: Oxford University Press, 1998), 13–14.

3. J. Edwin Orr, *The Fervent Prayer* (Chicago: Moody Press, 1974), 5–6.

4. Charles Finney, "Lecture 8: Meetings for Prayer," in *Lectures on Revivals of Religion*. Web. 17 June 2009.

5. Dietrich Bonhoeffer, *Life Together* (San Francisco: Harper & Row Publishers, 1954), 49.

6. Bonhoeffer, 87.

7. Bonhoeffer, 86.

8. C. H. Spurgeon, "Prayer Meetings," 526.

9. Francis A. McGaw, quoted in Captain E. G. Carre, ed., *Praying Hyde* (Gainesville, FL: Bridge-Logos, 1982), 54.

10. Leslie K. Tarr, "The Prayer Meeting That Lasted 100 Years," *Christian History* 1, no. 1 (1982), 18.

11. As quoted in "The Moravians and John Wesley," *Christian History* 1, no. 1 (1982), 28.

12. C. H. Spurgeon, *Morning and Evening* (Peabody, MA: Hendrickson Publishers, 1995), 281.

Chapter 6: The Practicality of Prayer

1. Adapted from J. Sidlow Baxter by Robert J. Morgan in *Moments for Families with Prodigals* (Colorado Springs, CO: NavPress, 2003), 152.
2. Ben Patterson, "Whatever Happened to Prayer Meeting?" *Leadershipjournal.net*, Web. 1 October 1999. http://www.christianity today.com/le/1999/fall/9l4120.html.
3. David P. Beaty, *An All-Surpassing Fellowship* (Grand Rapids, MI: Reformation Heritage Books, 2014), 73.
4. C. H. Spurgeon, "Renewing Strength," in *The C. H. Spurgeon Collection* (Rio, WI: Ages Software, 1998–2001), 29:897.
5. As quoted in Donald G. Bloesch, *The Struggle of Prayer* (Colorado Springs, CO: Helmers and Howard Publishers, 1988), 131.
6. As quoted in *The Kneeling Christian* (Peabody, MA: Hendrickson Publishers, 2006), 21.
7. As quoted in Kevin Adams, *A Diary of Revival* (Nashville: Broadman and Holman Publishers, 2004), 60.
8. E. M. Bounds, *The Complete Works of E. M. Bounds on Prayer* (Grand Rapids, MI: Baker Book House, 1998), 338.
9. Francis A. McGaw, quoted in Captain E. G. Carre, ed., *Praying Hyde* (Gainesville, FL: Bridge-Logos, 1982), 38–40.

Chapter 7: At Home in Prayer

1. John Newton, as quoted in Ruth Bell Graham, *Prodigals and Those Who Love Them* (Grand Rapids, MI: Baker Books, 2007), 41.

2. Ruth Bell Graham, *Prodigals and Those Who Love Them*, 39–42.

3. John Newton, "Begone Unbelief," in *The Olney Hymns* (London: W. Oliver, 1779), no. 37.

4. Quoted by Phil Anderson in *The Lord of the Ring* (Ventura, CA: Regal Books, 2007), 92.

5. Quoted by Leland Ryken in *Worldly Saints: The Puritans as They Really Were* (Grand Rapids, MI: Zondervan, 1990), 239.

6. Cheri Fuller, *When Couples Pray* (Colorado Springs, CO: Multnomah Publishers, 2001), 13.

7. See Genesis 2:24; Matthew 19:5; Mark 10:8; 1 Corinthians 6:16; and Ephesians 5:31.

8. Fuller, cited in *When Couples Pray*, 12.

Chapter 8: The Teamwork of Prayer

1. Terry Teykl, *The Presence Based Church* (Muncie, IN: Prayer Point Press, 2003), 18.

2. Edward McKendree Bounds, *The Possibilities of Prayer*, from *The Complete Works of E. M. Bounds on Prayer* (Grand Rapids, MI: Baker Book House, 1998), 165.

3. "The Empty Seat," in *The C. H. Spurgeon Collection* (Rio, WI: Ages Software, 1998–2001), 25:54.

4. C. H. Spurgeon, *Only a Prayer Meeting* (Geanies House, Fearn, Scotland: Christian Focus Publishing, 2000), 19.

5. *An All Around Ministry: Addresses to Ministers and Students, The C. H. Spurgeon Collection* (Rio, WI: Ages Software, 1998–2001), 231.

6. Daniel Henderson, *Fresh Encounters* (Colorado Springs, CO: NavPress, 2004), 59.

7. Quoted by C. H. Spurgeon in *Only a Prayer Meeting*, 19–21.

8. John Newton, "Public Prayer," *Fire and Ice: Puritan and Reformed Writings*, http://www.puritansermons.com/newton/newton4.htm (accessed June 23, 2009).

9. Charles G. Finney, Lecture 8: "Meetings for Prayer," *Lectures on Revival of Religion*, 122. Web. 29 July 2009.

10. C. H. Spurgeon, *Only a Prayer Meeting*, 17.

11. Jonathan Edwards, *Works of Jonathan Edwards*, v. 5, edited by Stephen J. Stein (New Haven: Yale University Press, 1977), 322–27.

12. Kathryn Teresa Long, *The Revival of 1857–58* (Oxford: Oxford University Press, 1998), 103.

13. William Wilberforce, *The Private Papers of William Wilberforce*, edited by A. M. Wilberforce (London: T. Fisher Unwin, 1897), 201.

Chapter 9: Lessons Learned from a Praying Past

1. John Pollock, *Moody* (Grand Rapids, MI: Zondervan, 1967), 232–35.

2. Interview by *The Preacher and Homiletic Monthly*.

3. Michael Green, *Sharing Your Faith with Friends and Family* (Grand Rapids, MI: Baker Books, 2005), 34.

4. C. H. Spurgeon, *The Sword and Trowel*, January 1865 in *The C. H. Spurgeon Collection* (Rio, WI: Ages Software, 1998–2001), 13–14.

5. Ibid., 32–33.

6. C. H. Spurgeon, "Ask and Have," vol. 28, *The C. H. Spurgeon Collection* (Rio, WI: Ages Software, 1998–2001), 686.

7. C. H. Spurgeon, vol. 5 of *Spurgeon's Expository Encyclopedia* (Grand Rapids, MI: Baker Book House, 1984), 30–31, italics mine.

Chapter 10: More Than We Ask or Imagine

1. John Piper, *A Godward Life* (Sisters, OR: Multnomah Publishers, 1997), 115, emphasis added.
2. Quoted by Robert O. Bakke in *The Power of Extraordinary Prayer* (Wheaton, IL: Crossway Books, 2000), 129.
3. Jonathan Edwards, *An Humble Attempt to Promote Explicit Agreement and Visible Union of God's People in Extraordinary Prayer for the Revival of Religion and the Advancement of Christ's Kingdom on Earth*, vol. 2 of *The Works of Jonathan Edwards* (Peabody, MA: Hendrickson Publishers, 1998), 292.
4. Ibid., 291.
5. Bryan Chapell, *Praying Backwards* (Grand Rapids, MI: Baker Books, 2005), 29–30.
6. E. M. Bounds, *The Complete Works of E. M. Bounds on Prayer* (Grand Rapids, MI: Baker Book House, 1990), 153.
7. *The Kneeling Christian* (Peabody, MA: Hendrickson Publishers, 2006), 44.
8. Donald G. Bloesch, *The Struggle of Prayer* (Colorado Springs, CO: Helmers and Howard Publishers, 1988), 76–77.
9. Quoted by E. M. Bounds in *The Weapon of Prayer* in *The Complete Works of E. M. Bounds on Prayer* (Grand Rapids, MI: Baker Books, 1990), 443.
10. Bloesch, *Struggle of Prayer*, 78.
11. C. H. Spurgeon, *Morning and Evening* (Peabody, MA: Hendrickson Publishers, 2000), 617.
12. Chapell, *Praying Backwards*, 167.
13. C. H. Spurgeon, "The Preparatory Prayer," vol. 56, *The C. H. Spurgeon Collection* (Rio, WI: Ages Software, 1998–2001), 9.

Sources

Books and Articles

Adams, Kevin. *A Diary of Revival*. Nashville, TN: Broadman and Holman Publishers, 2004.

Anderson, Phil. *The Lord of the Ring*. Ventura, CA: Regal Books, 2007.

Bakke, Robert O. *The Power of Extraordinary Prayer*. Wheaton, IL: Crossway Books, 2000.

Baldwin, Joyce G. *Esther*. *The Tyndale Old Testament Commentary*, vol. 12. Leicester, England: InterVarsity Press, 1984.

Bennett, Arthur, ed. *The Valley of Vision*. Edinburgh, Scotland: The Banner of Truth Trust, 1975.

Blackaby, Henry, and Claude V. King. *Experiencing God*. Nashville, TN: Broadman and Holman, 1994.

Bloesch, Donald G. *The Struggle of Prayer*. Colorado Springs, CO: Helmers and Howard, 1988.

Bonhoeffer, Dietrich. *Life Together*. New York: Harper and Row Publishers, 1954.

Bounds, Edward McKendree. *The Complete Works of E. M. Bounds on Prayer*. Grand Rapids, MI: Baker Book House, 1990.

Carre, Captain E. G., ed. *Praying Hyde*. Gainesville, FL: Bridge-Logos Press, 1982.

Chadwick, Samuel. *The Path to Prayer*. Sheffield, England: Christian Literature Crusade, 2001.

Chapell, Bryan. *Praying Backwards*. Grand Rapids, MI: Baker Books, 2005.

Cymbala, Jim. *Fresh Wind, Fresh Fire*. Grand Rapids, MI: Zondervan Publishing House, 1997.

Edwards, Jonathan. *The Works of Jonathan Edwards*, vols. 1 and 2. Peabody, MA: Hendrickson Publishers, 1998.

Fuller, Cheri. *When Couples Pray*. Colorado Springs, CO: Multnomah Publishers, 2001.

Gesswein, Armin. "Jesus Builds a Prayer Meeting." Web. 28 July 2009.

Graham, Ruth Bell. *Prodigals and Those Who Love Them*. Grand Rapids, MI: Baker Book House, 2007.

Green, Michael. *Sharing Your Faith with Friends and Family*. Grand Rapids, MI: Baker Book House, 2005.

Hallesby, Ole. *Prayer*. Minneapolis, MN: Augsburg Fortress Press, 1994.

Henderson, Daniel. *Fresh Encounters*. Colorado Springs, CO: NavPress, 2004.

Henry, Matthew. *Commentary on the Whole Bible*, vol. 4. *Christian Classics Ethereal Library. www.ccel.org/*.

Hybels, Bill. *Just Walk Across the Room*. Grand Rapids, MI: Zondervan Publishing, 2006.

Long, Kathryn Teresa. *The Revival of 1857–58*. New York: Oxford University Press, 1998.

Morgan, Robert J. *Moments for Families with Prodigals*. Colorado Springs, CO: NavPress, 2003.

Murray, Andrew. *With Christ in the School of Prayer*. Gainesville, FL: Bridge-Logos Publishers, 2002.

Newton, John, and William Cowper. *Olney Hymns*. London: W. Oliver, 1797.

Olford, Stephen F. *Lord, Open the Heavens*. Wheaton, IL: Harold Shaw Publishers, 1962.

Orr, J. Edwin. *The Fervent Prayer*. Chicago, IL: Moody Press, 1974.

Osbeck, Kenneth W. *Amazing Grace*. Grand Rapids, MI: Kregel Publications, 1990.

Piper, John. *A Godward Life*. Sisters, OR: Multnomah Publishers, 1997.

Pollock, John. *Moody*. Grand Rapids, MI: Zondervan Publishing Company, 1967.

Richardson, Albert Ernest ("Unknown Christian"). *The Kneeling Christian*. Peabody, MA: Hendrickson Publishers, 2006.

Ryken, Leland. *Worldly Saints: The Puritans as They Really Were*. Grand Rapids, MI: Zondervan Publishing Company, 1986.

Spurgeon, Charles Haddon. *The C. H. Spurgeon Collection*. Rio, WI: Ages Software, Inc., 1998–2001.

———. *Morning and Evening*. Grand Rapids, MI: Hendrickson Publishers, 1995.

———. *Only a Prayer Meeting*. Geanies House, Fearn, Scotland: Christian Focus Publications, 2000.

———. *Spurgeon's Expository Encyclopedia*, vol. 5. Grand Rapids, MI: Baker Book House, 1984.

———. *The Sword and Trowel*, vols. 1–7, in *The C. H. Spurgeon Collection*. Rio, WI: Ages Software, Inc., 1998–2001.

Tarr, Leslie K. "The Prayer Meeting That Lasted 100 Years." *Christian History* 1, no. 1 (1982): 18.

Teykl, Terry. *The Presence Based Church*. Muncie, IN: Prayer Point Press, 2003.

Web Page References

Chewter, G. "The Church Prayer Meeting, Its Decline and Revival." Posted July 16, 2004. *Banner of Truth. banneroftruth .org*. Accessed July 22, 2006.

Finney, Charles. *Lectures on Revival*. Published 1868. *Christian Classics Ethereal Library. ccel.org*. Accessed July 29, 2009.

Patterson, Ben. "Whatever Happened to the Prayer Meeting?" Posted October 1, 1999. *Leadershipjournal.net. christianitytoday .com/le/1999/fall/9l4120.html*. Accessed July 4, 2006.

Acknowledgments

I will remain grateful all of my life to Garth Rosell and Robert Mayer for their unflagging faith in this work. Joel Collier, your "bloodhound nose" for interesting historical anecdotes helped keep me on the trail. Thanks also to Kerry Skinner, Harris Campbell, and Devin Bell for their practical insights and to Steve Witte for his quiet encouragement along the way. I am indebted to David Beaty, pastor of River Oaks Church in Clemmons, North Carolina, for his thoughtful input (including the "Prayer Guidelines" in appendix 8). I also owe Walter Herrin of Duncan, Oklahoma, and John Strong of Holtville, California, a debt of thanks for first pointing my feet to this path.

To Miranda Gardner, Judy Markham, Annette Gysen, Katy Pent, and the rest of the creative and supportive team at Discovery House and Our Daily Bread Ministries—what a blessing it is to work with you! Words cannot express my gratitude to God for you and for your vision for this book.

Peace Church of Durham, North Carolina—your prayers have kept the vision for this project fresh. Bruce Gray deserves a medal for kindly plodding through early drafts without complaint. Heartfelt thanks also go Cheri Fuller, Terry Teykl, Jon Graf, Star Parker, and Dr. Bill Wilson for your thoughtful consideration of the unedited manuscript.

Daniel and Jordan Henderson, your encouragement and exemplary instruction in worship-based prayer has been an incredible blessing. I'm also grateful to the Durham Ministers in Prayer group for your faithful perseverance these last fifteen years. Don Westbrook, Dub Karriker, Dick Bigelow, Mac Bare, Wade Bowick, Scott

McClintock, Dupsy Omotosho—you have sown seeds in prayer, and the harvest is coming. May we see it soon!

Cari, my wife, what words would suffice? Without your encouragement and vision this book would have remained a file on my laptop.

To God above all—Father, Son, and Holy Spirit, Savior, Redeemer, Advocate and Friend, the One True Light coming into the world—be praise, thanks, and adoration forever! This book belongs to you, Abba Father. May it be used for your glory.

About The Author

Dr. James Banks's books have encouraged many people to pray. He is the author of *Praying Together, Prayers for Prodigals, Praying the Prayers of the Bible, Praying the Prayers of the Bible Perpetual Calendar, Let's Pray* (Discovery Series), *Prayers for Your Children*, and the *Praying with Jesus* DVD. James is also a writer for *Our Daily Bread*. James and his wife, Cari, have been married over thirty years and make their home in Durham, North Carolina, where James is the founding pastor of Peace Church. They have two adult children. James is a much-loved speaker at conferences, retreats, churches, and special events. For more encouragement in prayer and for information about hosting an event with James, please visit JamesBanks.org or search for his author Facebook page.

Note to the Reader

The publisher invites you to share your response to the message of this book by writing Discovery House, P.O. Box 3566, Grand Rapids, MI 49501, U.S.A. For information about other Discovery House books, music, or DVDs, contact us at the same address or call 1-800-653-8333. Find us online at dhp.org or send e-mail to books@dhp.org.